To Morgan
from Chris.

Kent's Care for the Wounded

Sept. 2020

KENT'S CARE FOR
THE WOUNDED

KENT'S CARE
FOR THE WOUNDED

BY

PAUL CRESWICK, G. STANLEY POND

AND

P. H. ASHTON

WITH A PREFACE BY

SIR GILBERT PARKER, BART., M.P.

(Hon Col Kent Royal Garrison Artillery)

All Profits on Sale given to the Kent County War Fund

HODDER AND STOUGHTON
LONDON NEW YORK TORONTO
MCMXV

INTRODUCTION

No nation in the world has the capacity to impro-
vise and the will to compromise so thoroughly as
Great Britain, and these characteristics have never
been shown more fully than during the past ten
months; that is, since the Great War began.
There is in the British nature a curious instinct of
freedom which, in its highest expression, has made
Great Britain the mother of freedom in government in the world, and in its lower form makes
anything like iron discipline imposed by any force
outside the individual himself more than difficult
to apply. The instinct of every British man is to
think for himself, act according to his conscience,
fear God and honour the King; but he does not
easily lend himself to what has been called " mili-
tarism " in civil life. No doubt he carries that to
an extreme, and organization on an extensive
scale is, therefore, difficult in ordinary times. Yet
his habit of thinking for himself, and of assuming a

personal responsibility, enables him to recover lost balances in crises like that produced in August, 1914. Given the crisis and the need, action is not long delayed, and the Englishman can produce marvels of improvised organization in a quicker time, with more skill, and with a greater basis of solidity than any man anywhere in the world. That he has the defects of his qualities is unhappily apparent, because he fails to appreciate organization for long purposes and for far-reaching ends; but when once he gets going, as it were, when once he begins to organize for his accepted purposes, he keeps on and on with endless persistence.

It was well known that the Red Cross Society and the Order of St. John of Jerusalem had an efficient and well-tested organization, that they were filled with enthusiastic, capable and skilful workers; but they were not organized for a war like the present. However, the same earnest, far-seeing souls who realized that a great European war might come, did something to prepare for the crisis and arrange a nucleus of purposed effort by establishing Voluntary Aid Detachments in connection with the Territorial Force.

I do not think that enough credit has been given

to those who originated this idea, or to the enthusiastic people in Kent and elsewhere who worked, long before there was war, in preparation of hospital work by trained amateurs, with all the multifarious, difficult and intricate duties attached to Field Hospital and Rest Hospital work in war-time. At the beginning there was the usual half-contemptuous chaff, and even sneers, at hospital amateurs, as there had been at Volunteers and Territorials, by those who believed that only the long-term discipline of regular service could produce effective and skilful organization, units and individuals. These people forgot, as they always do, that amateur assistance is drawn from the most intelligent and the best classes of the community, with a sense of responsibility, and with voluntary desire to accomplish a purpose behind; which makes up to a considerable degree for a lack of those prodigiously valuable qualities of the professional in the army and in hospital work. There was criticism; there was jealousy; there was even belief that the Voluntary Aid Detachments, when they were formed, were only playing at hospital work; and when war broke out even responsible people said that they would not be employed for nursing at all, or, if employed, their hospitals would only be Convalescent Homes. All that disappeared like mist before the sun. Just as the great political parties in the State composed their differences and compromised with their prejudices in order to produce an active national administration, so the British Red Cross Society and the Order of St. John of Jerusalem amalgamated for war purposes, and the professional hospital began to act in sympathy with and to give encouragement to the V.A.D. hospital.

I can speak for what happened in Gravesend where we have two V.A.D. Hospitals, where representatives of the general hospital sit upon the Executive of the V.A.D., and assist, advise and co-operate in every possible way.

No better evidence of the capacity for initiative and for improvised organization may be found than in the work done by the Voluntary Aid Detachments in Kent County, under the Presidency and control of the Earl of Darnley. When he assumed the responsibility the War Office were not absolutely clear as to the extent to which the Voluntary Aid Detachments could be entrusted to do responsible hospital work, and the detachments themselves were only groups of partially trained amateurs in nursing and war-work, though the commandants had shown skill and enthusiasm in organizing and training their detachments. There was even discouragement " from above " as to making ready hospitals for receiving and caring for patients. This did not deter the detachments from making due preparation of hospitals in the certain anticipation that the War Office would use them at a very early date. Many detachments believed that their skilled services would be called upon very soon, when it was remembered that the hospital organization of the army was only devised for, at the most, 300,000 men. While wiseacres deprecated the preparation of hospitals, and while the Voluntary Aid Detachments were advised in responsible quarters to abstain from opening hospitals, yet in places like Gravesend, common sense and ordinary prevision decided upon a policy of making hospitals ready. This was done ; and not a moment too soon, for, on October 13th, a command came from headquarters to mobilize all hospitals in Kent. But the Voluntary Aid Detachments were not taken unawares and responded efficiently to the call. The account given in this book, admirably written, and arranged interestingly, reads like a charming piece of fiction, though it is but a tender tract of truth, full of enthusiasm, vitality and graphic description. It is no fancy picture, but represents British initiative and improvisation, British energy and character at its best. And as to the work done, the fact that the War Office has, since October, continually sent patients to the V.A.D. hospitals in Kent, sometimes even crowding them, is good evidence of their national usefulness and of good things accomplished. Lord Darnley and his organization may well plume themselves upon the commendation given by such hospital experts as Colonel D'Arcy Power, whose letter to Dr. Yolland on April 27th (quoted in chapter VIII) is a certificate of which the Kent V.A.D.'s may well be proud. Sir Frederick Eve, Advisory Surgeon to the War Office, has also given his warm commendation; but the warmest commendation comes from the patients themselves, who have continually praised the skill of the hospital staffs, and enjoyed comforts which have been most generously supplied.

This book is no dry account of work done by a gallant and efficient organization, it is almost a thrilling story of human effort, suddenly commandeered to perform both military and civil services ; an effort put forth with a capacity and whole-heartedness which makes the nation and the empire its debtor. I commend this book for its own sake to the generosity of the public, and I commend it for the cause to which the profits from the publication will go.

GILBERT PARKER

CONTENTS

CHAPTER VII

FOREWORD

To the County Director of the Kent Voluntary Aid Detachments.

Sir,

I am commanded by the Army Council to request that you will convey their cordial thanks to the Voluntary Aid Detachments in your command, more especially to those of the Dover and Folkestone Districts, for the able assistance rendered to the Representative of the War Office during the disembarkation and disposal of the sick and wounded Belgian soldiers, arriving during the period 12th to 16th October.

I am to state that the Council much appreciate the assistance rendered by all concerned, which materially expedited the handling of the large numbers of sick and wounded to be disposed of, and mitigated the discomforts which the Belgian soldiers were bound to suffer under the conditions then existing.

I am, Sir,

Your obedient Servant,

(Signed) B. B. CUBITT.

November, 1914.

KENT VOLUNTARY AID DETACHMENTS

I

HOW THE BELGIANS CAME TO KENT

"Three more here, please. Qu'est-ce que vous désirez? Avec votre ami? Mais oui, certainement. Can we squeeze in another? Carefully now. . . . Par ici, m'sieur—South Hill Wood Hospital; come back here again.

"Cot case? The Chief of Staff says Memorial Hospital? Bring the stretcher along to the ambulance car, keep the blankets over his feet. . . . Help them, you other bearers, will you? That's the idea. . . .

"Four more for the Masonic Hall; keep friends together as much as you can. Two here for the Dewey Ward, Cottage Hospital, and two here for St. Mary's——"

Scene, Bromley South Station, midday on Wednesday, October 14th, 1914—at the end of the up platform. Scores of motor-cars waiting along the "goods" roadway; a grey oppressive sky overhead, but the rain holding off whilst the first trainload of wounded and dishevelled Belgian soldiers was being detrained with hasty tenderness by members of the Men's Voluntary Aid Detachment. The nurses of the Women's Detachments had already refreshed the valiant travellers with draughts of hot coffee and Bovril, the ministrations and sympathy of these quick-witted smiling angels upon earth being just what the poor warriors needed so sorely. A memory must have come to them then, fraught with bitter pain.

All about us was a polyglot tongue : French, Flemish—the English which we always conceive to be the only language a foreigner can understand. But, somehow, folk made their meanings plain, the will to be of service was so irresistible.

Twelve hours earlier Bromley had been its half-sleepy self, a typical country town, rather conscious of its dignity, always eminently respectable, and consequently more than disturbed by those persistent rumours of all that Germany was doing to her very small neighbour. Ugly dreams, sleep-banishing dreams, although, like all our countrymen and women, we wanted to think them dreams —that, at the most, exaggeration was responsible for the greater part of these tales of horror and frightfulness. Now, within the span of a night, the whole town had been shocked into that action which shows us at our best. No Hymns of Hate.

The Kent Voluntary Aid Detachments had been steadily preparing for this hour. They had been mobilised late on the night of Tuesday, October 13th, and had at first scarcely credited the urgency of the summons. " A false alarm, just to see if we can live up to all we have professed. Just to keep us alert."

For years past the Detachments had been making ready; the members of the British Red Cross Society, St. John, and the Territorial Force, all vying with each other, and generally being smiled upon—tolerantly, by some people. These detachments were formed to be the link betwixt the Base Hospital and the Field for the Territorial Force Association in case of invasion. . . . Of course, we may never be wanted, most of us thought within our hearts, echoing the opinion voiced by those outside the movement. Invasion —isn't it *almost* inconceivable ? Still, we may as well go on, in case impossibilities happen. Anyway, we shall be ready if the call comes. At the signal, we can fall in.

All throughout England many Red Cross workers had acted in this fashion, gradually taking themselves more and more seriously, fortunately for the country. Attending lectures, drills, camps—Red

Cross manuals in our pockets, marching about country lanes with stretchers, sometimes carrying lazy pseudo-patients. Perhaps a trifle hard on long-suffering relations with our zealous bandage practising ! Since the declaration of war on August 4th, 1914, all of us more energetic than ever, those who could having joined the Army—not always the R.A.M.C. Others, not able to pass the very rigorous tests imposed in the earlier days of national recruiting, now serving to the best of their ability. Getting ready, *in case*. The whole history of our Voluntary Aid Detachments serves to demonstrate once again that everything in this life depends in the main upon intelligent anticipation.

On this mid-October grey day thousands of trained men and women—trained to discipline, to self-control, to knowledge (at least) of the elements of hygiene and home nursing—were " making good " all over England. In Kent, which had been mobilised as a whole county, nearly one hundred Detachments, each with its commandant, medical officer, quartermaster (and lady superintendent for the women), pharmacist and other personnel of all ranks, about forty to fifty, were active in a labour of love for which they had taken pains to prepare. The scene at Bromley South Station was being repeated at every considerable railway centre throughout the country. Within fourteen hours of the call, over two thousand soldiers, Belgians and British, were comfortably in their beds, safe under English roofs, being cared for in surroundings as pleasant and fragrant as only the true English woman can devise. Weary, heart-sick soldiers—many of them so utterly exhausted as to be beyond caring what happened to them, either for good or ill. Deep slumber presently bringing merciful oblivion to their unheard-of wrongs and anguish of mind.

Wonderful hospitals these of Kent—and merely examples of what is being done by the Red Cross everywhere. Yesterday they had been, possibly, not too beautiful village halls, public buildings, empty black-windowed houses, forlorn in the centre of wintry gardens. Church rooms and village clubs. To-day bright somehow sunlit palaces, cheery all through, properly equipped—looking as though they had been Nature's Rest Houses all their days. About them moved blue-garbed, white-aproned, sweet-faced women, quietly doing the work appointed to them by the doctor and trained nurses, the red-drill-clad commandant overseeing all, directing here, helping there—resourceful, able, never at a loss.

The whole atmosphere charged with healing and love. . . . One might well say (as in *The Way of the Red Cross*—the eloquent story of a great movement told by E. C. Vivian and J. E. Hodder Williams) that not even the Genie of Aladdin's lamp could have brought about greater transformation.

II

A GLANCE BACKWARD

THE British Red Cross Society is successor to Lord Wantage's "British National Society for Aid to the Sick and Wounded in War," and the "Central British Red Cross Council." These were merged into one on July 17th, 1905, at Buckingham Palace, at the instigation of his late majesty King Edward VII, when the B.R.C.S. was founded and placed under the Presidency of her most gracious majesty Queen Alexandra. The Society was granted a Royal Charter of Incorporation, by Letters Patent, on September 3rd, 1908.

Lord Wantage's Society dated back to 1870, the "Central British Red Cross Council" came into existence in 1898. The earliest B.R.C.S. voluntary aid detachments are dated April, 1910.

Of the Order of St. John of Jerusalem it is only needful to state the fact that a "Hospice for the Entertainment of Wayfarers and the Reception of the Sick" was built at Hexton in Yorkshire *in the time of King Athelstan*, and was still in being in 1099. The sponsor of the Order was John Eleemon, a Greek Patriarch of great charity, of Amalfi, who founded a hospital at Jerusalem before the Crusades. This " Place of Entertainment for the Sick " had two thousand beds, and was founded in 1050. It was possibly the first true hospital ever known. The present St. John V.A.D.'s were founded in 1910.

The Territorial Force Association had a few detachments in Kent in 1914, these being practically drawn either from the ranks of the British Red Cross Society or the St. John Association.

All these detachments, as will be readily imagined, are much the same in their methods, aim and organisation. The main differences are practically those of uniforms and rank badges. All stipulate that a member must obtain a First-Aid Certificate from the ruling body of its Association ere being regarded as other than a probationer, and all examinations are held after study from (virtually) the same book—Dr. James Cantlie's universally known *First Aid to the Injured.* Members of women's detachments are required to qualify still further after a course of Dr. Cantlie's " Home Nursing " lectures.

Those in control of the B.R.C.S. and St. John detachments in Kent came into consultation, immediately upon war being declared, with the County Territorial Force Association at Maidstone, in order to discover whether the detachments

Photo by Daniels Bros., Lewisham.

A typical Kentish Hospital—all beds occupied.

could not be made even more useful on emergency. The Admiralty and War Office had long since agreed that all offers of voluntary assistance should reach them only through these Societies. The three administrative bodies in Kent, after a meeting at Maidstone in the very early days of August, 1914, decided to join forces for the term of the war, and the Kent Voluntary Aid Detachments, as we know them, were forthwith united under a single control. A series of meetings followed, culminating in an overflow assembly at Bromley Common on August 12th, at St. Luke's Church, under the presidency of Lady Northcote.

It seemed better that there should be one County Director rather than two, and eventually it was agreed that Dr. Cotton, Deputy Commissioner of the St. John Ambulance Brigade and County Director of the Territorial Force Association, should be nominated as the Kent Voluntary Aid Detachments' County Director, while Dr. Yolland, who had practically created the B.R.C.S. in the No. 1 division of the county, should be known as the Chief of Staff. The whole of the detachments were to be mobilised, when the signal should come, by the Territorial Force Association, under the presidency of the Marquis Camden.

Gifts and all manner of promises of support began to pour in at headquarters when these were opened at No. 53 Bromley Common. It was apparent that supreme efforts would be needed in order to deal with the new and vigorous growth of the Red Cross movement, and, in this connection, not enough can be said or written in praise of the organisation swiftly but surely built up under the whole-hearted guidance of the Chief of Staff. With his band of devoted workers he mapped out a complete plan of campaign, every detail being provided for and all contingencies foreseen. Dr. Cotton, who was most unfortunately taken ill soon after the scheme was well under way, still rendered much help by virtue of his great experience and knowledge, when, had he followed his physician's advice, he should have been taking complete rest. As a result, to the great regret of everyone, Dr. Cotton's health broke down, and, towards the close of August, he tendered his resignation, after having had the satisfaction of seeing the Kent V.A.D.'s established as a thoroughly sound business proposition.

At the suggestion of the Territorial Force Association the Right Honourable the Earl of Darnley, himself far from being in robust health, came forward patriotically to fill the gap. He took up the onerous duties on September 3rd with enthusiasm, labouring for the cause with tact and ability. Working closely with Dr. Yolland, who visited Lord Darnley almost daily at Cobham, progress was continued without a break—and, as there was no time to register the eager-to-work new detachments, these were, by a happy inspiration, allowed to carry on as individual " contingents " to existing detachments. Looking back, one can scarcely understand how all the vast quantity of work was got through in those days of the creation of the V.A.D. organisation.

Lectures had to be arranged, both for First Aid and Home Nursing. Medical officers all over the country came forward self-sacrificingly to give these, or take the consequent examinations. In the meantime everybody drilled, and prepared, and read-up, and practised.

The men's detachments, now drawn practically from those either too old for military service or already rejected (for some slight defect), found themselves able and thankful to be of service in the hour of need. New members filled the spaces left by those of military age who had gone to the Front. In this respect the St. John Association lost heavily, the members showing themselves most patriotic and determined, while the Red Cross Society took upon itself to see that there should be no consequent loss to the movement.

To each member of the women's detachments was given a list of articles likely to be wanted should a hospital be opened in the district; a most comprehensive list, drawn up by the hand of a genius. Articles of the humblest description were canvassed for by the ladies of Kent as well as those implying a more serious obligation. It was part of the scheme, and the finest part of it, that everybody should be able to help, from the highest to the lowest. Every promise received was registered, then all were classified—the addresses of all friends were territorially arranged so that the collection could be made with ease and dispatch. " Get ready—get ready " was the constant command— and soon there was a splendid array of promises of beds, blankets, mattresses—kettles, saucepans— every conceivable article that the hospitals were likely to need. Suitable buildings throughout the length and breadth of the county were urgently sought for, and, when discovered, were inspected and approved. Necessary structural alterations had to be put in hand, adaptations and improvements and extensions of existent village halls and other buildings. Luckily there were a few weeks available in which to perfect all plans, before the coming of that ever-memorable day for Red Cross folk of Kent—Tuesday, October 13th, 1914.

III

PAYING THE PIPER

It is neither our desire nor our intention to weary our readers by placing before them statistics, but it would be impossible to take a complete survey of Kent's care for the wounded without making some brief reference to the manner in which arrangements were made and carried out for placing the hospitals on a satisfactory financial basis.

When the Kent branches of the three Voluntary Aid associations amalgamated for the period of the war, it was generally recognised that the conversion of public and other buildings into temporary home hospitals and the cost of their maintenance would entail an expenditure over and above the sum realised from the daily allowance made by the War Office. Since that decision was arrived at, those who have visited any of the hospitals have had ample demonstration of the fact. One of the first things to be done, therefore, was to devise some scheme for raising a fund which could be used to supply such additional comforts and extra care as should be considered necessary.

It was perfectly clear that, in view of the many appeals which were being made throughout the country, the fund would have to be provided from purely local sources, and to that end an influential committee, representative of every part of Kent, was called into being under the gracious presidency of the Marchioness Camden. This Committee soon gave evidence that it was on business bent, and a most propitious start was made.

As we have before stated, a large and enthusiastic meeting was held in Bromley during the second week in August, when the fund was formally launched and an appeal made for £10,000. Mr. J. W. Wheeler-Bennett started the campaign with a handsome donation, and made a stirring appeal to the people of Kent, pointing out that the V.A.D. hospitals were legitimately entitled to a share of their generosity and benevolence.

It was soon found the right note had been sounded and that Kent was fully alive to its responsibilities in this matter. Everyone seemed so willing to give in money, service, or kind that at one time it seemed that there would be overlapping and confusion. This, however, was happily prevented by the circulation of an appeal from the Right Honourable the Lord Harris, Deputy-Lord-Lieutenant of the County, asking that all these most patriotic offers of financial and other assistance should be made through the Kent Voluntary Aid organisation, so that they could be directed into those channels whence the greatest good could be secured for the greatest number.

This appeal had the desired effect. Funds and stores were collected, and arrangements were made for the careful and systematic distribution of the gifts received. The readiness with which people gave showed that they were proud of their county, of their England, standing at the greatest crisis in all its splendid and romantic history. They remembered that our gallant sons had gone across the water not only to maintain the prestige of the " Union Jack," but also to fight under a banner on which are emblazoned in letters of gold the words " International Righteousness, Freedom, and Honour." Under these circumstances, the least that they could do was to put forth strenuous efforts for making adequate provision for the reception and treatment of the sick and wounded.

It was not long before the Executive Committee realised that the sum of £10,000 would be inadequate if the hospitals were to be maintained in their state of high efficiency and if the patients were to continue to receive those extra creature comforts which were the gifts of a generous public When this sum had been collected, therefore, the Executive Committee, with their customary prudence and foresight, decided to make an appeal for additional donations to the County Fund, in which endeavour the Marquis Camden gave a generous lead. The fund is being wisely administered ; and those who can see their way to assisting, can rest assured that the money available will continue to be profitably expended.

IV

THE CALL

It is a matter for cheerful reflection that we are necessary to the well-being and harmony of things, if this conviction can be reconciled with the persuasion that the sort of work we turn out is commensurate with a mighty need. Such reflections can be legitimately indulged in by the members of the Kent Voluntary Aid Detachments.

Let us remember that the success which is attendant upon their work is not the result of a few weeks' or months' activity. It is rather attributable to the fact that for years past many hundreds of women have been toiling unceasingly and heroically in an endeavour to obtain that degree of efficiency in nursing which should make their services valuable in the hour of their country's need.

Such women are the salt of the earth. If they were to sit still and fold their hands the wheels of the universe would seem to drag heavily.

When they were undergoing their course of training there were many onlookers who regarded it all as a huge joke and thought that they were but spinning worthless cobwebs for the remorseless housewife Oblivion to sweep away. But time alone can show the value of work and whether it has a worth beyond the occupation, stimulus, and interest which it furnishes to the minds of the workers.

People may make grand spasmodic sacrifices, but to maintain constancy without flaw or damage as the V.A.D. members did under the trial of criticism and sometimes ridicule is the best proof of fidelity. The dignity of their labours and the conviction of utility, coupled with the sedative and consoling reflection that at any rate they would be prepared for any emergency that might arise, enabled them to cling with unflinching tenacity to the task which they had set themselves. Having put their hand to the plough they would not turn back and indulge the world with the scandal of a deserted cause. This constancy and devotion to self-appointed duties compel everyone to admit that these noble women are unquestionably serving their generation to-day, and England is reaping the reward of their exertions.

When war was declared in August, 1914, and everyone's thoughts naturally turned to the dread possibility of long casualty lists being issued, it

was considered a very debatable point as to
whether the services of the Voluntary Aid Detachments would be called upon to any great extent.
But everything was prepared in readiness. Two
months passed by, and then came the summons
which brought home to the people of Kent more
forcibly than anything before the fact that England
was at war.

It was the night of Tuesday, October 13th.
The day had been a particularly busy one at the
headquarters of the Kent organisation, and the
staff there were contemplating retirement to a
well-earned rest, when a little after ten o'clock
came the already well-known sound of the telephone
bell. Slowly word by word the following startling
telegram was transmitted from the General Post
Office, London, and copied down to ensure ac-
curacy :—

"Mobilise all your hospitals at once. Notify
names of places, stations, and number of beds
available at each to transport officers, Folkestone. Large number of wounded arrive to-
night. Authority Director-General, A.M.S.

"COLONEL WILSON, S.M.O."

No longer could thoughts of sleep be entertained. The call had come, and over one hundred

commandants had to be communicated with and
told to summon their detachments into activity at
once. How was it to be done ?

A list of those officers who had the telephone
installed at their houses, or who had arranged to
receive messages through neighbouring houses so
provided, were promptly dealt with. That night
was a busy one at the Bromley Exchange, and
great credit is due to the operator there for the
splendid assistance which he rendered.

In some cases friends were sent in motor-cars
to waken the people, and in this respect Mr. J. W.
Wheeler-Bennett rendered a signal service. One
of the first arrivals on the scene, he went off
cheerfully with a long list of people in his possession
to whom the order had to be made known. It is
curious to note that at one house this well-known
and highly esteemed magistrate was suspected of
being a burglar, and it was some time before the
occupants could be convinced of their mistake.

Where direct telephonic communication was
not available the police authorities were called
upon, and they, too, did their utmost to ensure
the safe and prompt transmission of the message.
The replies which were received gave evidence in
many cases of the lateness of the hour. Considerable surprise was also evinced, and some of the
conversation was of sufficient interest, not un-

tinged with a degree of humour, to make it worthy
of record here.

" Mobilise the Detachment ? Oh, yes, I will do
it the very first thing in the morning."—" But
you must do it now."—" What ! to-night ? "—
" Yes, without fail."

" I'll let the Commandant know early in the
morning."—" But you must notify her at once."
—" But this is the vicarage."—" Very well, sir,
then I know everything will be in order."

" Yes, but I shall want a written order."—" A
written order, when wounded may now be on their
way ? "—" Is that so ? Then we will proceed at
once."

" Do you really mean *to-night?* "—" Yes."—
" All right ; you can rely on us."

" But everyone is in bed ! "—" Very well, go
round and pull them out."

" Oh ! I thought it would come in the middle
of the night. That's always the way.—But I'll be
out and about in a jiffy ! "

" What *will* the neighbours say ? But what-
ever they say, I will get the car out and have all
our folk up forthwith. Good-bye."

" Who is it wants me at this time of night ? "—
" Dr. Yolland." — " Yes, Doctor ? " — " Mobilise

your detachment and prepare your hospital."—
" Eh ?   What ?   Mobilise *at once?* "—" Yes, immediately."—" Right you are, Doctor, I'll get
round to them." The wire was responsible for a
prolonged yawn being distinctly heard. This,
doubtlessly, was the preliminary step.

As we have already seen, everything had been
prepared in intelligent anticipation of mobilisation ;
but, with so urgent and far-reaching a call, it
seemed possible that, even with Kent's wellnigh
perfect organisation, some of the wounded men
might arrive before all the beds were ready.
Wonders were wrought, however, well within the
margin of the strictly limited notice given to the
detachments, which, under the Mobilisation Order,
comprised those of the British Red Cross Society, the
St. John Ambulance Association, and the Territorial
Force Association throughout the county.

Church halls, parish rooms, and other buildings, all somewhat desolate - looking on a mid-
October night, were one by one transformed
into cheery, warm, and extremely comfortable
wards. The rooms were brightened with flowers
and with the smiles and smart uniforms of the
ladies, who had, in company with scores of willing
workers, toiled unceasingly from the moment of
the summons.

Among those who most generously gave up their homes, wholly or in part, for use as hospitals, and who, in many instances, are also contributing the whole or a large portion of the cost of maintenance, are Lady Hillingdon, Lady Sargant, Mrs. Ashley Dodd, Mrs. Coombe Baker, Mrs. Vining, Lord Darnley, Mr. T. C. Dewey, Sir Robert Laidlaw, Dr. Ireland, Mr. Wythes, Sir Everard Hambro, Mr. Bennett Goldney, M.P., Mr. H. M. Rogers, Mr. A. H. Squire, Mr. Boyd, Mr. Gurney Preston, Mr. George Marsham, and Major Powell-Cotton.

In the result, long ere the hospital-trains steamed into their respective stations, everything was more than ready. Thus, one of the greatest triumphs of voluntary civil organisation was completed to the very last detail.

V

ONE OF MANY VIGILS

" TRAIN being dispatched with about 150 wounded men to-night—arrive before twelve.—Disembarkation Officer, Dover."

It was at seven o'clock on Sunday, November 6th, 1914, that this telegram was received. Plenty of time to arrange everything, for we had a possible 200 beds in view. The telephone was kept going for about an hour ; by then our friends had promised us cars in plenty—our commandants were giving the finishing touches to new wards or completing the making up of further beds in wards not too full. The stretcher-bearers were mustered at the station by ten-thirty, fires were lit in the waiting-rooms. It was an awkward station from an ambulance man's point of view, steep flights of stairs led from the platforms with sharp turns right and left at the top of the flights into a glassed-in corridor. Then another turn into the booking-hall.

Many discussions went on as to the best way of

negotiating these obstacles to quick and safe transport. The members of the men's detachment opened and closed stretchers, opened them again and, after the orthodox testing of each opened stretcher, coaxed light-weight members to become temporary patients. These, duly blanketed, were carried not over-solemnly up and down the steps; sometimes the patient was carried head first, other times legs first—according to the imaginary wounds.

Nurses arrived with more blankets, alighting from cars in which were tea-urns, huge jugs of coffee, bottles of Bovril. These were lifted in, and further debate arose as to the best possible spot for the creation of an impromptu canteen. The ladies settled the matter by deciding to be on the end of the up platform, near by the foot of those still unlovely stairs. "The train *must* come in on this platform and we shall be able to look after every patient as he passes by." The stationmaster said that the train might draw up on the down platform. You never knew, and it was Sunday night, and the down road was open. If there were other hospital trains for London, following ours, the up road would have to be clear.

"They'll have to be switched on to the down line, and then switched back again when they're past us," decided the Commandant—which the station-master agreed was a reasonable plan. He decided to enquire at the signal-box.

Twelve o'clock drew nigh ; then left us, still patient. A thin rain, driven by easterly winds, began to find out weak spots in the detachments. A sharp stretcher-drill was given to the men by a keen quartermaster : up and down the platform —never mind the rain ! The ladies decided to move the canteen a tiny bit nearer the platform waiting-room, where a brisk fire burned in the grate. The motor-car owners and chauffeurs assembled in the booking-hall, stamping their feet and rubbing their hands together. " Any news of the train ? "

The station-master, returning from the signal-box, answered with a shake of his head : " Nothing yet, sir. I'm afraid it hasn't started."

" But it's nearly one o'clock ! "

" Great deal of dislocation at the Dover end, sir. They're sure to wire."

Irrepressible member of the stretcher-bearers sees his chance. " You don't wire dislocations, station-master. You have to deal with the joint first. Get it back through the capsule——"

"Fall in, there!" snapped the ubiquitous quartermaster, suddenly lighting on these two. " Section-leaders have their men on the platforms, for foot drill. Fall in, sharp."

The rain passed away, the air grew appreciably more chill. A luggage-train jolted along the down road, banging and groaning. Laden with equipment, khaki-coloured field guns—all manner of unusual goods : " You're not supposed to see any of these things," said the station-master. " They'll go through all night, now they've started. A regular procession of them." A dim notion of England's stupendous need—her supreme adventure, came to us.

" Last Sunday night I couldn't get to sleep for the din," opined one of the bearers, taking advantage of a brief " stand at ease—stand easy."

" It was the Russians going through, I expect." This from the Irrepressible.

" We shan't be able to use the down road now. You gentlemen will have to be quick when the train comes."

" When is it coming, Station-master ? "

" No news yet, sir."

Nearly two o'clock. Past two o'clock. Very much " fatigue " parties required to make up the fires. Porters busy in the porters' room, behind closed doors. " And I don't blame them, either," decided the Irrepressible, annoyingly wide-awake. " I never want any sleep ; but if I did——"

" You could go to sleep unloading wounded

from hospital trains ? " asked the quartermaster bitingly.

Half-past two. Some of the ladies more than quiet in the waiting-room beside the again brisk fire. Three o'clock. " Any news, Station-master ? "

" Just had a wire to say she's left Dover, sir."

Lightning calculations on the part of those whose brains were yet active : " That means nearly five before she arrives."

" Left Dover at 2.49, sir, the wire says."

" It'll be five all the same," declared a pessimist suddenly assertive.

" You're always on the cheerful side, you are. I remember what you used to say about the Red Cross. Broomstick Brigade, you called us. Jolly glad to come in when we'd let you, though."

" I always said that, given certain eventualities, the Red Cross was a splendid movement," complained the pessimist, unmistakably hurt. " Of course, I didn't expect the Germans would fight us, after all."

" When I remember the splendid spade-work done by our Chief of Staff—done unselfishly, unsparingly, at all seasons for the last five years— and when I remember how he has been supported by the Red Cross women of Kent, who have made themselves *able* to do the work they're doing so splendidly. When I remember the gratitude of

Photos by H. Palfrey Harman, Bromley.

the poor chaps we've already brought in, and how they've been cared for and nursed and rewarded in some little way for all that they've done for us, and when I recollect that some people used to laugh at our Chief—not openly, because they were too polite—but laughing really, and regarding him as a good fellow utterly mistaken—you know what I mean——"

The speaker checked himself. " I get carried away when I get a view of what duffers some of us were. How blind ! Never thought the Germans would fight us after all, eh ? Wasn't it lucky one of us could see ! Lucky one of us could have the nerve to go on. Just think what Kent is already doing, and imagine what Kent *will* do, now that our organisation is perfected. A crusade, indeed ! I'm humbly grateful not to be too old to take part in it. Do you fellows know that some of these men here, these stretcher-bearers, have paid for others to take their duty so as to be able to attend drills and lectures ? In peace time, too ! Drawn from all ranks ; they're postmen, gardeners, clerks, employers, big City men. Some of them come to drill in their motors, others with their tools in a bag across their shoulders. Fall in ! They're all comrades at once. *And* the women ! God bless them—as the soldiers bless them, for all their love, and tenderness, and patience, and cheerfulness. Merry hearts that go all the way. They didn't 'fall in' in their present order without having trained, and studied, and kept at it for years past. See them working in the hospitals, see them down here losing their night's rest—but going on duty to-morrow, despite all that. No grumbling——"

The speaker seemed quite ashamed after this outburst. But there was nothing to be ashamed about. He had talked it " off his chest "—and felt better. Everybody agreed with him—and he had lightened the weary waiting. So we forgave him magnanimously for being a—man of Kent !

Four o'clock. Four-thirty. The continuous procession of heavy, mysterious luggage trains had almost ceased to interest. It was certainly a very long night. Some of us yawningly fancied we could distinguish dawn in the eastern sky ; others declared for a late moon. But all disputing ended with the vision of the station-master signalling from down the line with his red lamp. " She's coming—she's round the bend. Hear the brakes ? Hurry them up with the coffee ; tell the bearers to stand by. She's in—jingo ! mustn't the poor beggars feel absolutely worn out ! "

Then a strange scene for this country platform, under the flickering, sighing gas lamps. A sad scene, one to make angels weep . . . the sweet

veil of early morning obscured the very worst. . . .
But the pity of it ! . . . " Jealousy cruel as the
grave "—never truer words in the Book of Books.
The outcome of bitter jealousy in this piteous
procession of yet living testimonies to a ferocity
far worse than that of beasts of prey. These our
brothers—behold them, shamefully wounded, foully
injured, scarce covered in their rags and mire; their
homes, so laboriously builded, now a mass of red
and smoking ruins; their wives and little ones——

It does not bear remembering, the ending of our
vigil; one of many, which, strange enough at the
outset, are now part of the ordinary routine. It
only bears remembering how, under Providence,
we were able, in our clumsy fashion, to comfort
them a little, and be, for once, men and women
less utterly unworthy of having been made in His
likeness.

VI

STORIES

"You cannot understand the feeling one has when the order comes for you to leave the trenches to capture those of the enemy," said an iron-grey Seaforth, discussing the eternal subject with the Commandant of the cheerful little hospital in which this quietly brave fellow had been a patient. He was a Territorial, an old "London Scottish" who had joined the 4th Seaforths immediately upon the call. An "old bachelor" as he called himself; keen, well-educated, experienced—but in saying he was thirty-nine one could not hurt his feelings. Rather the contrary!

"To anyone of imagination it's rather awful," he went on. "I'm not a coward. At least, I have never thought of myself that way until we had the order. . . . You know then that it's Death who may be whistling for you. You can't help fearing that you're taking an odds on chance of being smashed, of becoming unidentifiable, of being flung into an anywhere grave. Nobody to know any more about you, until—— Well, perhaps never. Reported missing.

" Somehow, you find you're out of the trenches, plunging forward over scarred, horrible ground, not the sweet earth you've known, but the land of a nightmare. The air about you full of bleak noises—that deafen, yet don't take away your sense of hearing. Some of this infernal row is coming from yourself : you're screaming yourself hoarse and don't know it. You see your pals shot down either side of you, bullets go singing by your ears—the big guns roaring behind are as dangerous as those of the other fellow's. Your own artillery —we had thirty fifteen-inchers, so they said—is shelling the enemy's trenches for you, as a preliminary. They're timed to cease fire just as *you're* timed to arrive. Some of our men were a bit too previous.

" Few things go exactly right, you know," he added. " Young Elliott. . . . Well, it had far better have been me. He's an only son, public-school boy ; fine chances before that lad. And he wasn't spoilt, nor likely to be. Things threw us together whilst we were at the depôt at Bedford, and afterwards, too, — ' Somewhere in France.' He had put in for a commission, but, after we got to know each other—— You see, I'm too old for rank. . . . A lovable chap who could act like that——

" We were side by side at the beginning of that

D

mad race; then he drew ahead, younger legs and a bigger courage. He was first man in the German trenches at Neuve Chapelle. I like to talk about that, although you've heard it often enough from me. Then, one of our own shells came screeching.

"I got there, amid all the scrimmage and din. Jumped down on top of a German who was stooping over something. He seemed to go out, like the flame of a candle—blown out—puff! I don't recollect quite what happened, only that presently we had cleared the trench. Three hundred in that trench and only seventy-five were taken prisoners. There was a kind of zigzag communication to the next line of trenches; our fellows—Fourth Army Corps, you know—were being shot down fast as they got to the opening. I saw one of 'Ours' get through, at last; then I got stuck in the back—a flesh wound, but it stung! Rotten luck! The slush at the bottom of those trenches was pretty bad. Thought I should choke in it. But, even so, I wasn't afraid any more. Only angry, sick with anger. When they brought me into the hospital it was just the same.

"We were in the base hospital for one night. Heavy fighting, heavier casualties. 'Get 'em across to England fast as you can.' So we came to Dover and waited long hours at the Disembarkation Office—and I remembered that boy every minute.

Could see him, you know, just as he jumped the trench. . . . I've told you about that, haven't I? We hadn't a notion where we were going; but, soon as we detrained, there was young Elliott. . . . Being carried by two of your bearers. It was good to see him, although——

"Someone helped me to him, and I caught hold of him. Anyhow,—just to feel he was safe home. . . . They let us go together in the same car, and we came to you. We have been very happy here, and you know we're grateful. But now I'm at the end of my furlough and going back; while young Elliott's crippled and deformed for the rest of his days.

"It might have been much worse? That's so. What I mean is, that if it had been me it wouldn't have mattered so much. He is a youngster, whereas I've had something of a fling. . . . You'll tell him I called? That I'm jolly glad he has been able to go for a drive? To-morrow I'll be in France again, but I'll write. You might say to him that I'll write for certain sure. That I won't forget. . . . He'll understand."

Another story comes from a Leinster. An un-exploded bomb fell in the trench. It meant one man's life, or many. So he disobeyed orders and climbed out of the trench, with the bomb clutched against his breast. It exploded as he was flinging it from him, both hands held above his head to get better impetus. He has two fingers only on his right hand now; only the use of his thumb on the left. " If I hadn't thought to hold it high I'd be a dead man this day. So I would. And if I tould 'em it would lose me a good conduct stripe for disobeying order-rs! I'll have to learn to work with me feet—but I'll not be the first to do that. There was Cassidy, the Arumless Wonder. I see him play cards with his toes, the blessed creature, and shuffle the pack like a Christian. And fire off a pistol and all."

Another—from a Belgian soldat de Ligne. Rheumatism—through standing in water-logged trenches for nearly a week. He had been *garçon de café* in the Boulevard D'Anspach at Brussels before the war. A conscript who, after a week's rough training, had fought like a veteran for the honour of his outraged country. He had a little house in the suburb of Uccle, near by the Hôtel Terminus. Had been swept across to England from Antwerp in the great rush of mid-October, 1914, utterly unable to get news of his home and family. One afternoon in November, whilst dragging himself along the High Street under the gentle escort of a Red Cross " orderly," our patient suddenly uttered a cry of joy, and, losing hold of his

Photo by Nettle, Beckenham.

Early Morning in the Ward.

crutch-stick, fell forward into the arms of his wife
a refugee, brought by miraculous chance to a
Bromley home.

One more—from a Lincoln this time—told as
he was being motored across to the military hospital, to be discharged to furlough. " Four of us
brothers there was, sir—two of us wounded like
me, and one killed in action. Not a bad record.
And my sister's husband—that's my brother-in-
law, you understand—he's going out this week.
There's good work out there, sir—something to be
done. And mighty good fellers doing their bit.
A fine life, if you look at it the right side up. I was
on the reserve, but, bless you, we didn't need no
second summons. Four of us, and one's killed.
Had his back to the wall in Saint Eloore, and fell
face forrard. Plenty of pluck in young 'Erb. I
left another great pal o' mine there, too—dead on
the field. Saunders was his name—a good 'un as
ever breathed. Funny thing, last Monday afternoon, just about tea-time, somebody comes asking
for me at the door. I goes to meet him—and—
didn't I think it were a ghost! There was old
Saunders, alive and well. You bet I wasn't half
glad. Bullet went clean through him and knocked
him flat. But hadn't done no harm. You take
my meaning ? Funny thing they should bring him

to the little hospital other end of the town, wasn't it ? He asked if there was any other Lincolns, that's how he found me. He come from the military hospital where we're going, only last Monday—to what they calls convalesce. A small world, ain't it ? "

This is not properly a story, but an account given to one of our officers by a Canadian concerning his part in the attack at Hill Sixty. It seems that they were drilling, more or less peacefully, some way behind the fighting. " Having a stand-easy, sir, with a little refreshment—it being long after tea-time. Suddenly we heard a great shouting over and above the noise of the guns, and, looking round, we saw the Frenchmen running back to us from their trenches. Little black and blue dots, growing into men, and more men : shouting, crying, and calling out to us. What's the matter, what has happened ? Something about their guns, that's what they're saying. The sergeant called us up smartly. In a minute or so he had his orders, too : we were to join the rest and go forward. The French got into order again ; their officers stopped the shouting and sent them to the rear trenches. The Germans had collared some guns ; had rushed them under cover of gas-poison. We couldn't rightly make out whose guns they were, whether British, or Belgian, or French. Anyway, they were gone —and we had to go after them. . . . We made the attack at about two o'clock in the morning, the guns having been located at a farm close to a little wood. Artillery, high explosive, prepared the way, but there wasn't quite enough of it—and the big guns were in strength. Four battalions of Canadians—Queen's Own, Toronto— and others ; but not many got back. It did seem strange, that charge across the fields, dark and cold, with a blowing rain ; all sorts of queer frightening noises, too. The Germans soon spotted us, but we were well spread out in skirmishing order. We got through the entanglements pretty well ; they hadn't had time to properly fix them. Then a big blaze shot up, some sort of coloured fire —to help them find us. I saw the farm against the trees, saw our men running forward. We didn't make too much fuss, just running clumsily along. We had our packs, blankets, everything—you couldn't get much of a move on. It seemed wonderful I wasn't hit ; I remember thinking how very wonderful it was. The bullets were singing all over the field. . . . Presently a machine gun rattled out—but our boys were through. Noise enough then, regular pandemonium. Just as I reached the wood—smash went my arm ! Like a dry stick breaking. . . . Dropped my rifle, and down on my knees! First I gave up—lost my nerve. Thought I was dead. Laid in a ditch by the side of the wood for a bit; then tried to crawl along. Had to get rid of my pack, and could only use my left hand. The other felt numbed, very queer—not exactly pain, or else pain too bad to be felt. You understand that, sir? And the noise going on, groanings, and cries and whistling reports. Lights flaring; then wet darkness. I crept along the ditch for about a mile. Full of water and filth it was. I managed to find shelter in a little outbuilding, and stayed there till morning. Wondering about my wound—couldn't tell whether it was really bad, or not. My wrist and hand were all swelled like the dropsy. I managed to get back into our lines, and heard that our boys had spiked the guns as they couldn't get them home. And the wood and the farm were no man's land. Leastways, no living man was there. . . . Scarcely a third of our fellows left—but they had done their bit. The Germans won't forget the Queen's Own, Toronto. . . . I'm going along fine, thanks. Shattered wrist and forearm; it's all written on that little board top of my bed. I'd like to have seen the end of the fight. Bad luck, after being so close in at the finish."

Something about the gas fumes—from a 2nd Seaforth: " I was in the rear trenches. Sniping all day—some of those Germans can shoot! Ye can't put your cap on the end of your rifle and hold it up, without they'll score a bull. Macfarlane was a King's man, though. He had shown them some very pretty shooting that day from the first trench. But we were tired, ye ken. It was near ' relief,' and a steady wind blowing from the south-east. Mac had taken a peep to see whether we had long to wait. There's a fog coming, he passes the word; about the last he spoke. There was something wrong, we soon knew—and I made bold to climb up. There it was, green thick smoke, rolling along low down over the ground like a laddie bowls his hoop. About the height of a man's breast, and clinging to the earth, sinking into the trenches like water almost. I got a whiff of it and fell back, my eyes streaming and my throat all dry. It gets a grip of ye. The rear trenches didn't feel the worst of it, and we were able to do some fighting. They didn't have it all their own way. Many of them died in our trenches, thinking they would take them so easily. I got a cut through the leg; don't know how it was. It looks ugly, but doesn't signify now any more than at the time. The ambulance fetched me away, but I didn't want to go, although I couldn't see.

At the base they gave me sea-water to drink, and made me sick. And saved my life. My lungs feel it yet ; but if you could have seen the poor fellows lying dead, as I did see them. They do it this way, sir. The gas is in phials and they put these phials along the top of the advanced trench. When the word comes, they take out the stoppers and make a dash for the trench behind them. The gas rises up out the phials, and the wind blows it. Turns your inside all to water and froth ; kills all the grass and everything it touches. Doctor here has given me some medicine that's doing me good. But I had only a whiff, you must understand. Macfarlane was the grand marksman ; it's a pity and a shame he's gone in such a poor fashion. He was with me all through the South African Campaign, and always a bonny fighter, to say the very least. A brave kindly man that played fair all his life."

VII

A GARDEN HOSPITAL

NOT very far from the coast of north-east Kent, swept by its bracing air, yet sheltered by a ring of great trees from the first chilliness of our English winds, is that rest house for the sick which Kent knows as the Garden Hospital. A field road approaches it, but lamps are placed along the curves of this pleasant way, which can be lit, or extinguished, at will of the engineer in the power house. After you leave the field road the " way " winds under the belt of trees and brings you round into one of the fairest gardens in all the Garden County of England. In the early Spring, masses of primroses and violets show through the decayed fallen leaves of last Autumn, as you pass the tree enclosure—the garden itself is a series of stretches of velvet lawns banked by high beds of herbaceous plants and shrubs, which already are more than promising the wealth of Summer. Gay auriculas mingle with the white and purple arabis bordering the beds : near you is the rosery, the standards and dwarfs pruned, but breaking through in a manner which almost defies late frosts.

A long many-gabled typically English country-house faces the garden. An oak-roofed hall leads you by a gallery staircase to that part of the house still occupied by the generous owners : to the left of the spacious oak hall are the other halls, high-roofed,—the two large enough to provide floor space for forty beds. The owner is a big game hunter, and these " museums " were filled with the mighty framework of the great beasts he has captured. Were filled—now all are removed, or covered up—close-stored against the walls : neat plain-framed iron bedsteads, furnished with whole-some linen, and each covered with dainty bed-spreads of pink and blue, line the halls. A few huge palms throw across the passage ways of these great halls their spreading umbrella leaves—the roof is glassed in ; the place is beautifully warmed with radiators, which can be regulated to a nicety. A tiled floor, along which strips of matting are placed in the bed aisles, makes for thorough cleanliness combined with silence. Such are the Garden Hospital wards ; removed from them yet easily accessible, is a kitchen replete with every modern contrivance and staffed by capable devoted women who undertake willingly this part—perhaps the most important part—of Kent's care for the wounded. For this is one of the outstanding features of its crusade, the commissariat department.

Dr. CHARLES COTTON

A liberal weekly menu is arranged, so that variety may induce appetite. This rule applies all over the county, and very instructive are the housekeeping bills when they come before the Committee—as they do once a month. As a whole, the provisioning is most capably done—now and again a quartermaster's personal leanings are indicated. At least, so think the Committee!

At the Garden Hospital all is very methodical. The staff are just as gently enthusiastic as when they commenced work in October. Even in the Autumn the garden was very pleasant between showers—the paths being well made, hard, and soon dry, while many of the trees are evergreen. The dahlias were followed by border chrysanthemums, then, in all the sheltered spots, pure white Christmas roses opened their waxen petals. In the conservatories " show " chrysanthemums lasted until the end of January : a few of these were brought into the wards each morning and removed at dusk. There is an " entertainment " room, provided with a piano, all the newspapers, the inevitable gramophone, and free tobacco and writing materials.

The medical officer reports many wonderful cures from the Garden Hospital, so that now it is being used much more as a convalescent home— that many may benefit rather than a few fortunate ones, as were allocated there in the first rush. A large annexe has been fitted up, near to these literally scores of acres of land and gardens, and cosy woods ; the staff has been increased, so that the nurses and orderlies may occasionally have a little " time off " for their own relaxation.

Apart from all their unostentatious kindness the owners arrange much of the transport of wounded for the district, marshalling a fleet of cars whenever necessary. In this they are whole-heartedly supported by their friends and neighbours. Everybody in Kent is anxious to help, and more than willing to help when asked—which is not always the same thing !

It is not remarkable that few patients desire to leave this hospital, even when entirely restored to health and strength.

VIII

THE THEATRE

A FEW words here on a typical operating theatre. Kent has supplied many of these, and all the greater V.A.D. hospitals are thoroughly able to carry a case right through to convalescence. Kent has the best of trained advice—let that fact be clearly and emphatically stated. Trained nurses, either salaried or unsalaried, as their position and they themselves demand; and the best and most modern surgeons that the country has produced. These are at our disposal at all hours. One has to state facts plainly, sometimes.

The theatre under review is truly but one of many; well equipped, beautifully hygienic, and properly warmed. Conveniently adjoining the ward—no long draughty corridors to be traversed whilst the patient is being brought in. Complete X-ray apparatus, the latest in sterilisers, instruments and methods of administering anæsthetics. An overhead light by day, perfectly shaded lighting for night: everything orderly, systematic, and as right as human tenderness and ingenuity can devise.

Shrapnel and bullet extractions, trephining, radical cures for hernia, resetting of fractures only hastily attended to on the field, amputations when necessary, are all performed without any hitch. All dressings are aseptic in Kent hospitals, and kept so—injections are made on the most recent plan: the serum is received in small bottles with a rubber elastic cap, which when pierced allows the needle to draw up the fluid; when the needle is withdrawn the puncture automatically closes. This is the Mulford syringe.

After the first month it was ordered that no Belgian soldier should be sent to Folkestone for return to service unless he had been twice inoculated against typhoid. In many hospitals this was done by the medical officer of the detachment with perfect success. The risk of tetanus also is similarly guarded against — in fact our V.A.D. hospitals are second to none in equipment or the ability to deal with any contingency.

The following letter from Colonel D'Arcy Power is a testimony valued highly by the detachments, as, in the opinion of this well-known and eminent surgeon, it seems we have succeeded in attaining the point at which we have aimed—to have, at least, *deserved* our success.

" 10A, CHANDOS STREET,
" CAVENDISH SQUARE, W.
" *April 27th*, 1915.

" DEAR DR. YOLLAND,

" I have, as you know, seen much of your work in the Kent Voluntary Aid Detachments round Bromley, and I have operated in your improvised theatres. The work you have done and are doing is excellent. The essentials of success are with you ; cleanliness, a good water supply, willing service on all hands, and a capable supervision by trained nurses. The operative results, therefore, have been satisfactory, whilst the general condition of patients with wounds has been so good that they rapidly become convalescent. It is difficult to speak too highly of the sacrifice of home and comfort which has been made, not only uncomplainingly, but even with enthusiasm, by those ladies who have placed their houses unreservedly at the disposal of the patients for months at a time.

" Yours ever,

" D'ARCY POWER."

Sir Frederick Eve, Advisory Surgeon to the War Office, has frequently inspected the Kent V.A.D. hospitals, and has also expressed himself as thoroughly well satisfied with them.

E

CHAPTER IX

A KITCHEN

WE touched so lightly on the Commissariat Department in a previous chapter that we feel justified in devoting a page or so to this very important feature of the work.

For this purpose we will take you on a flying visit to one of the hospitals. Five o'clock in the morning! The distant horizon is just becoming tinged with a brightness which indicates the approach of day, as we arrive at a large and conveniently situated building over which a flag bearing the emblem of the Geneva Convention is faintly seen.

Passing under the portico, the door is opened to admit us into a spacious hall, a side-passage from which brings us to that part of the building which is customarily haunted by appetising odours. The scene which strikes the eye on entering the kitchen is one of neatness and precision, suggesting that everything is comfortably to hand.

The nurses are just entering upon the preparation of breakfast for some fifty patients, and

66

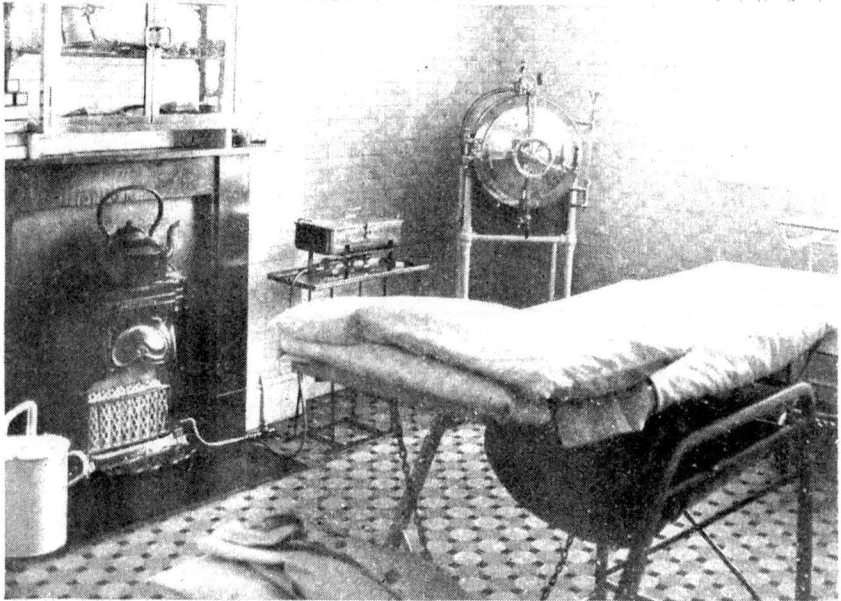

"Those now in

" on the Land . . . "

The Hospital Kitchen.

son, Ramsgate

Photo by Lambert, Fenchurch

their deftness of movement and generally brisk appearance give no evidence of their eight hours' vigil.

Here one is cutting up loaves of bread and spreading the slices with rich-looking butter which seems to tell of green fields gaily besprinkled with clover heads. There crockery, shining in its spotlessness, is being arranged on numerous trays in readiness to be circulated in the wards ; and rows of teapots, milk-jugs, and sugar-basins are being placed ready to contribute their contents for the production of that time-honoured beverage which, on account of its invigorating properties, is so welcome in the early morning.

Some time having been pleasantly spent in watching these operations, we now hear sounds issuing from other parts of the hospital, which show that the patients are stirring and preparing to break their fast. This is the signal for numerous eggs to be placed in a large pot of boiling water, and for large pots of jam and marmalade to make their appearance.

The minutes have passed quickly owing to the interesting information which the nurses have imparted in reply to our many and varied enquiries. Some shreds of the conversation are worthy of repetition here.

Do the patients appreciate their meals ?

Oh, yes, they seem to thoroughly enjoy the food, and they never make any complaints.

They certainly ought not. At what time do they have dinner?

One o'clock. But each man has either cocoa or milk at half-past ten. Directly the breakfast things are washed up and put away the day staff come in and commence preparations for dinner.

What is the general menu for the midday meal?

Those patients who are on ordinary diet have meat, two vegetables, and as much pudding as they desire.

What kind of puddings?

Mostly plain ones made with plenty of eggs and milk, and all the ingredients are of the very best quality. You can quite understand that the morning is fully occupied here in getting everything ready—for there is also the special dietary to be considered. Some of the patients have to be very cautiously fed.

Is tea provided?

Yes, at five o'clock. They have bread and butter, with cake or jam, and sometimes both.

That is the last meal of the day?

No. They have a light supper at half-past seven. What do we give them? Oh, various things. Bread and cheese with cocoa, soup, or fish-cakes.

We hurry away after being allowed to inspect a nicely arranged and well-stocked larder. But we carry with us very happy impressions of the Commissariat Department of a V.A.D hospital. From a dietary point of view at any rate these men have an enviable time. Let us take just a peep into the large ward before passing out. What a happy family! We leave them to their repast, mentally congratulating the Commandant and her Staff on the splendid management—and on the fact that the expenditure here is kept within the limits of the Government capitation grant of two shillings per day.

CHAPTER X

ORGANISATION

THE Kent Voluntary Aid Detachments have been put to the test. They have justified the high hopes always held of them by those who have seen the labour of past years. They have become very much more than their original modest ambition, which was to be of use in case of invasion. The Kent V.A.D. are, at the moment of writing, practically a voluntary Royal Army Medical Corps, fulfilling precisely the same ends and purposes as that distinguished body. These two are now almost one and indivisible; it is difficult to say where either begins or leaves off. The R.A.M.C. is responsible for all removals; whilst, at the request of the Eastern Command, the Kent V.A.D. remain under the Territorial Force Association for administrative purposes, under their County Director. The three great Military Hospitals in Kent—the Royal Herbert Hospital at Woolwich, Fort Pitt at Chatham, the Military Hospital, Shorncliffe—are the three centres, staffed and controlled by the R.A.M.C. To these

Taking advantage of the Sunshine.

Photo by De Ath and Dunk, Maidstone.

the Kent V.A.D. Hospitals are attached in their
respective groupings, and to these three they pay
allegiance. Our hospitals have become auxiliaries
of these centres, taking overflow cases, or receiving
convoys direct as ordered. All maintenance claims
are rendered through the parent hospital, all
admissions are notified to it; all British discharges
are made through it. The Belgian soldiers are discharged either to Folkestone, for immediate service
abroad, or through the Legation in London if unfit
for service.

In the early days of mobilisation the Red Cross
hospitals, acting under instruction, sent away
many hundreds of convalescent Belgian soldiers to
homes all over Britain. The transport in this
matter was something to remember—by those who
had to carry it through. It seemed good to the
authorities that that part of the Belgian Army
which was temporarily *hors de combat* should be
distributed throughout the length and breadth of
the country. Collecting these strangers in a strange
land in small numbers from widely separated
hospitals in order to make them up into parties
worth sending to such homes as the Lady Forester
at Llandudno, the Soldiers' Home at Dunoon,
homes so far afield as Kenneth Mont, near Aber-
deen, and Shouldham Court at Yeovil, and a dozen
other places—was a task which one does not lightly

forget who had any part in it ! The trains to be stopped at certain stations, the extra carriages to be provided, the anxiety of keeping your party intact all through the journey, with dozens of interested but rather bothersome folk ever ready to " stand treat " to the men the moment you were looking the other way ! The transport across London from South-Eastern termini to those of the other great systems ; the feeding of the poor fellows on sixteen-hour journeys. . . . These are things to remember all your days, if you have the duty of escorting and organising.

Discharges are now all British, and are made through the portals of the three military hospitals, emphasising the fact that the V.A.D. hospitals are annexes, as already stated. They are under military law, and conform to it willingly ; they are open to surprise inspection by the military doctors ; they cannot transfer a patient from any one hospital to another without military permission. So closely allied are the R.A.M.C. and the V.A.D. that requests are now urgent for the latter to supply the former with nurses, who, once they enter one of the military hospitals, will cease to be voluntary workers, and will receive their pay with the rest of the military nurses.

What the V.A.D. have saved the country cannot be properly estimated. *Everything is voluntary.* The War Office pays, on an average, something under three shillings *per capita* per night, for food allowance—that is the sole and only charge on the National Exchequer.

That is practically " billeting " allowance ; and, for the first four months, the grant was but two shillings per man per night. This amount includes everything : dressings, medical stores, transport to and from the military base, the nurse, the doctor, and the whole organisation. Of course we have had our buildings rent free, rates and taxes have been remitted, other splendid advantages have been freely accorded by those able to help.

The doctors give a great part of their valuable time willingly and gladly to the hospitals to which they are attached ; ladies do orderly work, any work, apart from their nursing, to help along. Friends send in food and milk and a score of things to assist the commissariat. Thus each hospital manages to keep out of bankruptcy, although, when we had the smaller grant, some of our hospitals came perilously near to insolvency. The Kent County War Fund put them on their feet, and kept them there.

Each hospital knows what it can do, and each quartermaster strives in friendly rivalry with her neighbours in the county. When a hospital planned to run forty beds finds itself averaging about eighteen patients per day it is not easy to keep within the limits. Heating, lighting and general upkeep of the building is exactly the same whether there are eighteen or forty patients. To make the proposition a business one it is necessary to keep our beds filled.

The larger allowance of three shillings meets the case *only* if the beds are well occupied. Well occupied they are, when our soldiers are being cared for in them, and the Commandant's great desire is to be kept busy; a modest aspiration.

She likes to feel that she is doing her part. That is her reward. That is the reward of all who are honestly trying to be unselfish and rather better folk than they were. There is no conceit about this sentiment; for often they who enjoy it are almost unaware of the blessing which has come to them.

It hurts a little, sometimes, that thoughtless folk should say that our workers are well paid for what they do. It is not true, and the fact must be set down here plainly. *From the Kent V.A.D. County Director down to the Kent V.A.D. bearer no one person other than a few of the trained nurses receives pay for his or her service.* The word voluntary should be sufficient in itself.

A comprehensive plan has been adopted in Kent

in connection with Lord Robert Cecil's scheme for tracing, or obtaining news of, the missing of all ranks. A list is sent, periodically, to the Commandant of each hospital containing full particulars of the missing men. Any soldier of the same regiment who happens to be in the hospital is possibly able to supply information concerning the soldier about whom enquiry is made—information which, in many cases, has been of the utmost importance to the anxious relatives. Reports are made at once in such an event, and a visitor follows up the matter by tactful and careful questioning. These visitors have also the list for their district, and are continually going round the hospitals gleaning news which otherwise might never reach those who are waiting here in suspense. Sometimes the news is good ; on other occasions dread uncertainty is, at least, at an end. The visitor's position is scarcely an enviable one, but the duty is performed wisely and so kindly that the best is made of a difficult task.

The Detachments owe a very great deal to General Whitehead, Deputy Director Medical Service, Eastern Command. He has helped the V.A.D. in every possible way. His kindliness and patience have made the road smooth. To him and to Colonel Simpson at Woolwich, Colonel Haines at Chatham, and Colonels Wilson and Noding at

Shorncliffe and their staff the Kent V.A.D. are very deeply indebted. Much of the success of the undertaking is attributable to the wise, healthy, and ever-courteous treatment which the authorities have accorded to Kent in her great enterprise of tending the wounded and sick.

The central organisation of the British Red Cross Society at 83 Pall Mall, S.W., has ever shown itself ready to help and advise, upon application being made to its officers, and sincere thanks are expressed to these gentlemen for their unfailing courtesy. Each Red Cross detachment in Kent was accorded £10, upon mobilisation, by the central body, and most of the supplementary contingents received £5.

Each St. John detachment was granted £5 by their governing body.

These equipment grants were added to by the Committee of the Kent County War Fund; each Red Cross contingent receiving £5, each St. John detachment £5, and each Territorial Force detachment £10.

Lt.-Col. Wood Martyn, the secretary of the latter force, has shown the Kent V.A.D. the greatest consideration from first to last. He has helped the cause along in many ways, and has displayed sympathy with its aims from the outset. His duties have now devolved upon his successor, Colonel

toto by Oscar Harder.

Lt.-Col. A. WOOD MARTYN

Winch, who has already shown himself thoroughly interested in the detachments.

It is with great satisfaction that we record the service cheerfully rendered to the detachments by the Boy Scouts all over the county.

It is right to say that the Kent detachments owe their progressive success largely to the sympathetic and very friendly treatment accorded them, and their Executive, by all in this our effort on behalf of " Christian Service and True Chivalry."

XI

STORES

THE success of the Central War Fund for the hospitals prompted the present plan on which Kent's stores and supplies are also centralised. It will be recollected that, at the beginning of the war, each Commandant was furnished with a carefully thought out list of articles likely to be wanted, should a hospital have to be brought into being ; and it will be readily understood that the canvass of a neighbourhood frequently resulted in an abundance of one set of articles, with the corresponding shortage of another. Headquarters decided to accept all promises, and collect accordingly at the right moment—then to pool the superabundant articles at given centres. Each hospital contributing to its central depôt had the privilege of applying to that depôt for any other thing which the particular hospital required.

These central depôts were, in turn, attached to the chief depôt, and could apply there for all articles not in stock. The chief depôt had, and has, especial means of procuring the wanted articles;

it is situated near headquarters, and it is only necessary for us in Kent to ask in order to receive almost anything we need. Such is the spirit which animates our county.

In some parts of Kent a veritable epidemic of blankets occurred; in others the excess of gifts was manifested by a delightful deluge of crockery and cutlery. In yet another district came an avalanche of medical stores; a fourth centre was overwhelmed with sheets and bedspreads. Each Commandant took what she needed from her over-plus, and forwarded the remainder to the centre, with a request for those articles she lacked. The chances were that these had already arrived from another hospital; if not, the request was passed on to the chief depôt, where a complete register is compiled of all stores at all depôts. If the application could not be met at the chief depôt, those in charge knew precisely where to look for help. The Kent County War Fund is always available, if other means cannot supply the desired article forthwith.

As a general rule, it was found that the register at the chief depôt pointed the way. Blankets were wanted at Cranbrook, which had too many sheets? Faversham had a stack of blankets, but few sheets . . . a card from the chief depôt adjusted the matter, in the course of two posts.

The Stores Committee worked, and continues to work, on sound business lines. Every centre takes stock once a month and reports to the chief depôt. Literally thousands of articles have been redistributed in the manner shown, and every kind-hearted and generous friend of the detachments has the satisfaction of knowing that his or her gift has not only been received, but has been, or will be, used.

Nothing is wasted, so nothing is refused. All find a place of service somewhere, and, as even the best thing has the knack of wearing out, or being broken, the demand for upkeep is constant.

Very acceptable presents have latterly come to the depôts. Several cases of new-laid eggs from the Egg-collecting Committee in London : from overseas, bags of flour, cases of sugar, hundreds of tins of jam and treacle. Sides of frozen lamb ; dozens of frozen rabbits—splendidly welcome presents these, bringing joy to the breast of many a kitchen matron, keen to keep her bills within bounds. We are indeed grateful to the Australian Government who, through Mr. Fowne, of the London Chamber of Commerce, is sending these splendid presents to the sick and wounded. They have more than helped us along in Kent; for each gift has been sent so very modestly, and with such heartening messages of sympathy and goodwill.

Here is a list of Kent's storehouses, with the names of those who have administered them so ably and unselfishly: Main depôt, Bromley, Mr. T. Pawley and Miss Pawley. Central depôts: Ashford, Miss Knock; Canterbury, Mrs. Mason; Chatham and Strood, Dr. Skinner; Chevening, Miss Hall-Hall; Chislehurst, Miss Paterson; Cranbrook, Mrs. Tomlin; Dartford, Miss Dixon; Deal and Walmer, Miss C. Reid; Faversham, Mrs. Alexander; Gravesend, Mrs. Bruce-Culver; Maidstone, Miss Hills; Margate, Mr. Leon Adutt; Sevenoaks, Mrs. Walter Hay; Sheerness, Mr. H. Rayner Catt; Tonbridge, Miss Taylor; Tunbridge Wells, Miss Violet Moore. These ladies and gentlemen have had no easy task; there are no sinecures in the Kent V.A.D.—nor room for them. All has to be kept going; patients are passing in and out the hospitals all the while. It is for them that everyone labours; that those who have served may now find such rest and peace as we, in our sincere endeavour, can provide.

F

XII

COMPARISONS NOT ALWAYS ODIOUS

IT is sometimes well to compare, in quite friendly rivalry, your own methods with those of others working for the same ends. By this means one has the opportunity of learning, even more than of teaching—which is the spirit which should animate folk who want to be really of use in this world. The management of our smaller voluntary hospitals will be considered here in conjunction with those of our larger Rest Houses. Owing to the generosity of those who provide the former the housekeeping of both costs much about the same per man : in the ordinary course the larger hospital has manifestly a big pull over the lesser.

But management can effect wonders, especially if there be a little assistance from the owner and friends of the small hospital. This has been always unostentatiously forthcoming, and one of the fine features of Kent's care for the wounded has been the unceasing and self-denying kindness of those who are not among the most blessed with this world's goods. Few of us are able to offer a hospital complete, but many have been ready to give up part of the home, and have made the sacrifice with quite surprisingly successful results.

A typical small hospital has been given us by the surrender of the top floor of a square-built house, where four straightforward rooms open on to a decent landing: these rooms have been emptied of superfluous furniture; the floors have been covered with plain linoleum; three iron-framed, spring-mattressed beds have been placed in each ward—which just allows the regulation 900 cubic feet of air space to be enjoyed by each patient. A double washstand, a table, three chairs, a chest of drawers completes each ward. Upon the landing is a table upon which the dressings, etc., are kept under a cloth; a second table forms a serving-place and resting-place for the orderlies when bringing the meals to the wards from the kitchen below. There is a fair-sized garden for fine weather, and a capital morning-room on the half-landing, just below the wards, for rainy days. Only light cases are taken, so that the patients are generally well able to manage the few stairs from the wards to the morning-room, and vice versa. Twelve cases can be provided for—and, the house being on high ground, the cures have been really remarkable; all the more so from the fact that, in the earlier days, more serious cases had to be entertained.

The housekeeping is very well arranged; the Quartermaster buys in reasonable quantities, and does not order five tons of coal at the time when the coal merchants are squeezing unfortunate consumers rather more than usual! Nor does she go to the other extreme, and buy coals by the hundredweight. There is an " in-between " method upon which our little hospital works; a common-sense method. Fuel is dear; therefore they buy moderately, in the hope of a fall in price. Also they state the position to the local trades-folk, and find that one and all put them on most favoured nations terms. Neighbours want to help; they do not need to be asked or given encourage-ment. So much can be done with tact and a sincere " thank you very much " manner. The hospital under notice has been generously endowed by the owners, but it is the housekeeping with which we are concerned. It is admirably done, and is but an example of many others. The patients are well-fed, well-nursed, cared for under-standingly without too much discipline, but just enough.

There is always sufficient food for the morrow; a little over in case of emergency, but nothing that can be wasted. They do not " run out " of any-

An improvised Ambulance at work.

Photo by Pickett, Bexley Heath.

thing in this little hospital, yet never have large stores, with the consequent temptation to be too lavish.

It is something of an anxiety to run this hospital, the cheerful Quartermaster admits. She has to be always thinking about food. But she does so " with a good grace."

The larger hospitals have their cares also, for they must have always plenty of everything.

One hospital on the riverside has 100 beds, and has averaged 60 patients per night since October, 1914. Something of romance about this place ; a great deal of that sheer pluck which has always a glamour for those of us who exercise imagination. One needs to be imaginative to become truly creative, and to be able to steadily pursue ideals. Then, sometimes it happens that ideals are nearly encompassed.

The vision we have, as we write, is of a great grey building alongshore ; shabby before it was new, an effort of olden happy days wasting ; neglect and the accompaniments of neglect apparent everywhere. That was the framework upon which some devoted women brought their splendid energies to bear.

It seemed a rather hopeless adventure. Our plucky ones saw the possibilities, and set out to interest friends and make them see possibilities.

Had estimates from decorators; considered these prudently, went carefully through figures and measurements and suggestions and—got to work.

It's splendid of you all, said onlookers; it's tip-top practice—it's finishing your Red Cross education. You'll be quite all right for field work when you're wanted—after practice of this sort ! Scrubbing floors and cleaning down, are you ? Having the windows mended, the place once more made habitable, electric light installed, hot and cold water put on ? . . . No doubt the military will be glad to use the place for a headquarters ; for, of course, you will not have any hospital duty there, you know. You cannot expect it. . . . The military hospitals are too fully prepared for all contingencies——

November 15th, 1914, proved that these amiable optimists were prophesying vainly. The great grey building had been only just transformed into one of the finest " unofficial " hospitals in Kent when the summons came. That day the whole capacity of the hospital was taxed to help stem the flood of wounded men returning to England.

Everything in the hospital had been systematised. The wards had been allocated in blocks, each block with its complete staff. On the huge ground floor were the surgical wards ; on the first and second floors were other surgical and the medical wards. The housekeeping department had been thought out by the kitchen matron to the last detail. Hot soup was ready for the men as fast as they were brought in—food was prepared for those who needed it, according to the diet deemed necessary by the medical officer. Orderlies were soon bathing the men ; other orderlies were sorting out the discarded rags of clothes, keeping the best of these and labelling them for the sanitary authorities, who collected the parcels, for disinfecting, almost as quickly as they were made up. Not too nice a job this ; the unfortunate soldiers had come straight from the trenches, bringing with them parasites who were both numerous and very tenacious of life. It is not a pleasant thing to remember ; but it happens each time a convoy of wounded is brought in, and the destruction of these vile pests is a part of the organisation which has to be perfect.

After bathing, and purifying as far as was possible—for some of the cases were very serious —the men were put to bed, their wounds dressed more thoroughly. Sleep was the great restorer to the bulk of these poor travellers, and morning saw a great change for the better in most of them. But the whole staff of the hospital had worked right through the night ; making up the War Office returns in the bureau, preparing the breakfasts, ticketing each man's personal belongings and bestowing them safely—underclothes had been washed, boots had been cleaned and put in lockers with such part of the accoutrements as could be wisely retained. The medicines were prepared by qualified dispensers, whose services remain at command at all hours : extractions of bullets and shrapnel in the very bad cases had been performed within the four walls of the hospital. The theatre is fully equipped—for when friends saw that all this was not the dream of a few enthusiasts, but positively and actually a hospital able to treat wounded men to the expressed satisfaction of the military authorities, more money and help came along. Nothing succeeds like success—an old proverb exemplified once again.

The installation of this hospital was effected without any charge on the Funds, thanks to an infinity of intelligent devising and improvising certainly not surpassed by any other national effort. The running of the hospital cost the country 2s. per day per man for the first few months; then application had to be made for the larger grant of 3s. in order that nothing might be wanting. Sixty soldiers have been each day lovingly cared for and healed—for love heals perhaps more quickly than medicine. Nearly four hundred patients have passed through this great V.A.D. hospital in the six months which have elapsed since it was opened.

Another hospital, this time by the sea, is situated beautifully for our purpose. Here we have all the same elements for success in tending and healing the wounded. A well-arranged house on three floors, with a fine entrance hall, is planned out methodically into wards for officers, rank and file—medical and surgical, as the case may be. A splendid operating theatre is fitted with every appliance for the ultimate ease of suffering humanity : the best of medical care and skilled nursing is always ready ; plenty of windows, bringing air and sunlight and hope into tortured breasts, plenty of the best food, and plenty of kind bright faces and clever hands to comfort sad hearts and soothe away pain. The kitchens of both these hospitals are superb. No great hotel has better outfit or management. All is scrupulously clean ; the shelves and dressers are opulently provided with the impedimenta of cooking. Larders full. Steam heating throughout the building : hot and cold water at all hours, baths on each floor, a cheering all-day view of the Thames, or the Channel with occasional peeps of "somewhere" in France. A stirring breeze when casements are wide, but a friendly, healthy breeze, for all that. "Night air is NOT poisonous"

—one of the mottoes on the walls of the wards.
A very hard-working staff at both these hospitals.
The Commandant at one of them commences her
long day's duty by cleaning out her own small
office, believing in the principle of never asking
anyone to do that which you won't do yourself.
And the same " fine rapture " pervades the whole
company, and is ever sustained at high-water mark.

Close upon 10,000 patients have been now
admitted to Kent's Voluntary Hospitals, and the
care of the wounded has been ever the first thought;
all have sought to keep that idea steadily in view;
have tried to make it All and Everything that
Matters.   Sometimes one has to pull oneself up;
selfish thoughts try to push out of the way the
Right Thought :

*We are trying to help our country and those who
have fought for it and us.*

Evening in the Ward.

Photo by Dr. Ath. and Dick. Maid-tone.

WORK OF THE DETACHMENTS

TERRITORIAL FORCE ASSOCIATION

KENT VOLUNTARY AID DETACHMENTS

County Director :

THE RIGHT HONOURABLE THE EARL OF DARNLEY,
Cobham Hall, Cobham, Kent.

Chief of Staff :

DR. J. HORATIO YOLLAND,
53, Bromley Common.

Assistant County Directors :

Division 1. DR. STERRY, Riverhead, Sevenoaks.

DR. ALLAN, " Aldborough," Chislehurst.

,, 2. DR. G. A. SKINNER, 42, North Street, Strood.

,, 3. SURG. - COLONEL T. JOYCE, Shepherd's House, Cranbrook.

DR. TRAVERS, Maidstone.

DR. WATSON, Tunbridge Wells.

,, 4. DR. PRIDEAUX SELBY, Teynham, Sittingbourne.

,, 5. CAPTAIN GIBBS, Keppel, The Croft, Hastings.

Division 6. DR. DODD, Manor Road, Folkestone.

„   7. SURGEON-GENERAL F. H. BENSON, Greton House, Walmer.

(Rest of District).

DR. FRANK BRIGHTMAN,
Aspley House, Broadstairs (Thanet).

Private Secretary to Chief of Staff :

G. STANLEY POND,
" Derwent," Crown Lane, Bromley.

Transport Officer :

PAUL CRESWICK,
The Haven, Scott's Avenue,
Shortlands.

County Architect and Surveyor :

GRANVILLE STREATFIELD, Westerham.

County Secretary :

W. R. BRUCE-CULVER, Hope House,
Gravesend.

Divisional Secretaries :

ALFRED POPE, 77, Crown Lane, Bromley.

MRS. BRUCE-CULVER, Hope House, Gravesend.

WALTER NEVE, Castle House, Sissinghurst, Cranbrook.

DR. J. P. HENDERSON, The Hollies, Green Street, near Sittingbourne.

Honorary Commandants :

Kent 18. DR. CRAWFORD.

Kent 22. MISS SANDFORD.

Kent 28. LADY ROTHERMERE.

Kent 29. DAVID T. MILNE.

Kent 29. W. E. ENDERBY.

Kent 33. H. G. HOSKIER.

Kent 50. G. STANLEY POND.

Kent 52. ALFRED POPE.

Kent 54. P. H. ASHTON.

Kent 56. HON. MRS. NICHOLSON.

Kent 76. DE BARRI CRAWSHAY.

Kent 78. R. H. YOLLAND.

Kent 96. MRS. JOSEPHINE FISHER.

Kent 116. F. J. PILE.

WORK OF THE DETACHMENTS

(Odd numbers are the men's, the even represent the women's detachments)

KENT 1, DOVER. The detachment has seventeen members serving with the R.A.M.C. The other members have not yet had many opportunities of rendering assistance, but are standing ready for any emergency.

Commandant—G. PLATER.
Quartermaster—S. TUPPER.
Pharmacist—G. FOSTER.

Members.—D. Bean ; S. Blackman ; W. Blackman ; E. P. Boddy ; C. Buzan ; A. Claw ; J. Colthup ; J. Cullen ; L. Dadds ; E. Dawkins ; E. Fagg ; J. Foord ; Frank Fox ; Fredk. Fox ; G. Fox ; P. Goodiff ; G. Gore ; I. Harman ; L. Hobday ; F. Holmes ; F. Hopkins ; C. Humphrey ; C. Johnson ; W. King ; W. A. Knott ; G. Marsh ; J. Marsh ; W. Mayne ; H. Mills ; P. Nibblett ; A. Nye ; A. Pearson ; C. Petts ; I. Petts ; J. Petts ; E. Phillpots ; H. Pluck ; A. Potter ; F. Seath ; B. Solly ; H. Spain ; E. Stokes ; T. Walton ; I. Wilkinson ; P. Wright ; P. Young ; S. Young.

KENT 2, RAMSGATE, was formed from the Ramsgate Nursing Division of the St. John Ambulance Brigade and registered in 1910, being the first women's detachment in the county.

On the outbreak of war an appeal for funds was

circulated, and preparations made for opening a hospital.

Early in October, 1914, the Wounded Allies Relief Committee arranged for the reception of wounded Belgians, and took over the " Royal Sailors' Rest," which had been placed at the disposal of the Government by the British and Foreign Sailors' Society to be used as a hospital with accommodation for seventy-two beds. The hospital was quickly prepared, the greater part of the extra equipment being lent or given by the townspeople.

On October 10th the first Belgian wounded to arrive in England were received, followed by men from the Expeditionary Force.

324 patients have passed through the wards.

The Hon. Surgeons—Dr. R. J. Archibald, Dr. Grace H. Giffen-Dundas, Dr. E. Fisk, Dr. G. E. Halstead, Dr. R. G. Hicks, Dr. T. G. Styan—have willingly given their services.

Commandant—Mrs. A. Grummant.
Medical Officer—Dr. A. L. Johnston.
Lady Superintendent—Miss E. M. Smith.
Quartermaster—Mrs. F. W. Hinds.

Members —Margery Ayerst ; Ada Mary Ayres , Minnie Bartlett ; Edith Bevan , Bethia Blower , Mary Boyland ; Emily Burley ; Emma E Caswell ; Mary F. Chapman ; Mary E Church-Brasier , Winifred G Church-Brasier ; Margaret Culver , Bessie Deveson , Elizabeth Duvall ; Mary Ann Dunbar ; Alison Mary Eastgate ; Sophia Foster ; Nellie Halsey ; Annie Harker ; Frances M. Hogwood , Edith

Maria Hollingworth; Edith E. J. Hulgrave; Ellen Kate Ingram; Mary Helena Jarman; Florence Jeffery; Gertrude Leigh-Lye; Fanny Jane Long; Ada Harriet Martins; Lottie Wootten Mascall; Gertrude McMillan; Ada Maria Medland; Delcie Peall; Ethel Priestley; Nellie Philpott; Editha K. Potts, Christina Mary Romboy; Nellie Rose; Emily Matilda Rowe; Margaret Sale; Cares Sharpe; Jane Studham; Mima Charlotte Sutton; Clara Vickers; Rachel Weigall; Ethel L. Whittingham; Mary E. Williams; Kathleen S. Wolfe; Violet Isobel Wotton.

KENT 3, SITTINGBOURNE, was formed in 1908 from the local St. John Ambulance Brigade. Since the arrival of wounded soldiers the men of the detachment have been engaged first at Trinity Hall Hospital, Sittingbourne, acting as sentries, orderlies, and transport bearers, and afterwards at the new hospital at " Glovers," where they have carried on excellent work at all hours of the day and night.

Of the original members sixteen have enlisted, their places being taken by certificated men.

Commandant and Medical Officer—DR. W. H. S. NOBLE.
Quartermaster—L. R. DENCE.

KENT 4, WILLESBORO', has worked hard for years past, and is standing ready to act when called upon.

Commandant—MRS. POTTS.
Quartermaster—MRS. VALLINS.

Members.—Lily Banks; Winifred Brett; Alice Cotterell; Charlotte Crust; Susan Fermor; Elizabeth Flint; Mary Greenstreet; Jane Hall; Emma Hamblin; Matilda Samson.

KENT 5, WESTGATE-ON-SEA, was mobilised on October 14th, 1914, the members of the detachment being resident in the Isle of Thanet. The men have since that date been engaged in transport, orderly, and nursing duties at Westgate, and have collected large quantities of hospital equipment and sent many of their number to join the R.A.M.C.

The detachment owns a motor ambulance, fitted up and driven by the members.

Commandant and Medical Officer—
DR. A. F. STREET.
*Quartermaster—*SERGT.-MAJOR CORNELIOUS.

Members.—W. Bickerton, J. E Brett; G. S. Britton; H. Button; W. Cox; C. H Dixon; J. Docking; P. Dyke; C Enderby, G. Enderby; W Enderby, H. Faver; S Faver, J E Fight; J A. Gammon, S W Gammon; T. Gransbury, A T. Jarvis, D. Kinmont; J Kinmont; W. G Knight; J. Millard, J H. Pointer; T W. Randall, H Stewart, E. Thurley, A J. Venis; I. Venis; A. Q. Verlander.

KENT 6, SEAL, was raised in 1909 by the Honble. Violet Mills.

After war was declared a hospital was equipped at The Wildernesse garage, lent by Lord Hillingdon, with accommodation for twenty-four patients in two wards, and a fully equipped operating theatre, with X-ray apparatus. A converted motor ambulance carries four stretchers. The greater part of the hospital equipment has been provided by the Dowager Lady Hillingdon, the rest by friends in the neighbourhood.

There are also nine beds in a supplementary ward at The Wildernesse.

Commandant—JOHN POLAND, F.R.C.S.
Medical Officer—R. T. DICK, M.D.
Lady Superintendent—SISTER M. HOWES.
Quartermaster—MISS OLIVE L. BLACKALL.

Members.—Rose Ansell ; Anne Burroughes ; Pamela Burroughes ; Winifred Davys ; Jane Dennis ; Verena Hay ; Dorothy Higgs ; Susan Hill ; Lucy Horne ; Doris Matthews ; Violet Mills ; Dolly Monckton ; Bertha Moss ; Lois Norburn ; Millicent Paris ; Clara Pratt ; Annie Roberts ; Alice Smithers ; Renny Taylour ; William Toogood ; Elizabeth West ; Emily West.

Trained Nurses.—Sisters Bridges and Phipps.

KENT 6 (attached), KEMSING. St. Edith's Hall in the village of Kemsing has been in use as a hospital since mobilisation. Those interested in Red Cross work in the neighbourhood have generously supplied gifts both in money and kind.

The members of the detachment are working under the direction of two trained nurses.

Commandant—MISS WILKINSON.
Medical Officer—DR. CARNARVON BROWN.
Lady Superintendent—MISS WILKINSON.
Quartermaster—MISS WARING.

Members —Eleanor Covell ; Alice Dibblin ; Mary Fife ; G. Nancy Godwin ; Winifred M. Goldsworthy ; Maud Hodges ; Nellie M. Hooker ; Dorothy Riches.

KENT 7, FAVERSHAM AND DODDINGTON. The members of this detachment have been doing useful work at the Faversham V.A.D. Hospital, acting as orderlies and sentries and undertaking the transport.

The Commandant has also the duty of Divisional Secretary.

Commandant—DR. J. P. HENDERSON.
Medical Officer—DR. HARPER.
Quartermaster—MR. POTTS.

KENT 8, FOLKESTONE, was started in 1910, but, owing to this detachment not being at full strength at the outbreak of the war, the members joined Kent 30, Sandgate, and have been working continuously at the Bevan Home, performing excellent service at all hours.

Commandant—MISS SOPHIA M. HOPE.
Quartermaster—MRS. EASTER PHILLIPS.

Members.— Florence Carr ; Ann T. Clark ; Lily Edwards ; Gladys Jeffery, Irene Jeffery ; De Lasaux, Margaret Warburton

KENT 9, FOLKESTONE. On October 13th, 1914, the War Office asked the detachment to assist in unloading the wounded at Folkestone Pier, the ambulance men also going in charge of trains to many parts of the country.

The men rendered great assistance to the

wounded Belgian refugees landed from the "Amiral Ganteaume," and assisted in removing them to the hospitals.

The detachment has continually assisted the R.A.M.C. in conveying the wounded from Shorn-cliffe Station to all hospitals in the district, also assisting at the Manor House Hospital.

Commandant—F. A. ADAMS.
Medical Officer—DR. C. WOOD.
Quartermaster—J. G. STROOD.

Members —J. S. Allen ; H. T Baker ; H Biggs ; W. Burden ; G. Burtonshaw , H. Coppens ; W. B. Couchman , G. Ellin ; B. Epps ; H. J. Epps ; H. Evans ; A Gardiner ; A. Gregg ; T. W. Hobbs ; O. J. Horton ; C Huntley ; W. Huntley ; V. Jensen ; J. Kimber ; E. G. Kinnett ; E. N. Marsh ; S. Marsh ; H S Maxted ; J. McQuire ; E. Menpes ; F. B. Overton ; A. J. Page ; C. Peters ; C. Port ; G. Port ; J. Port ; J. Puchinger ; J. W Rumsey ; R. Sargeant ; J. Sharman ; E. J Smith ; H. E. Smith ; V. Thompson ; W. Thompson ; F. Towse ; R. W. Whyborn ; C. Yeates.

KENT 10, CRANBROOK, was organised in 1910 by Lady Gathorne-Hardy, the detachment being placed under Mrs. C. Duncan Murton, who was the first lady Commandant appointed in the county. On the outbreak of war the Vestry Hall was offered by the Cranbrook Parish Council and fitted up as a hospital, where demonstrations in hospital work and routine were given by trained nurses. On October 17th, 1914, the first wounded (Belgian soldiers) were installed. A few days after a further convoy was received, and the Drill Hall, lent by the Territorial Force Association, was at once put into commission. Contributions have been generously forthcoming. The Cranbrook troop of Boy Scouts have rendered great assistance.

Surgeon-Colonel **T. Joyce**, of Cranbrook, is Joint County Director for No. 3 Division of Kent, and to his tireless ability this division owes much of its success.

Commandant—Mrs. DUNCAN MURTON.
Medical Officer—Dr. ARTHUR SHAW.
Lady Superintendent—SISTER D. POLLEX-ADAMS.
Quartermaster—MISS TYE.

Members—Evelyn Bengough; Gwenda Bengough; Ethel Boileau, C. A. Bourne; Nancy Bourne; Mabel Bradbury; Edith Daynes, Phyllis Fricker; Ruth Naomi Fulbrook; Elsie Goldsmith, Jessie Grover; Annie Horn, A. W. Hudson, Vera Kinnear, Bertha Moore; Helen Mordaunt, Mildred Mordaunt; Alice L. Piper; Clarice Rumney, Rosina J Russell, Lucy I. Seaford, Ellen Spratt; Amelia K R Stickells; May Taylor, Charlotte Tye; Esther Wickham; Katharine E. Woodin.

KENT 11, ASHFORD, has been working admirably in connection with Kent 48 in opening and running the Ashford Hospitals. Although hard at work all day to gain their livelihood, the members have carried on the night orderly duties at the hospitals.

Commandant—REV. F. T. GREGG.
Medical Officer—DR. C. M. VERNON.
Quartermaster—E. E. WOOD.
Pharmacist—F. W. STEDMAN.

Members.—A. Argrave; H. Arthur; G. E. Back; R. H. Baldock; A. D. D. Banks; R. Barman; A. Barnes; A. Butcher; A. J. Butcher; F. Butcher; A. J. Capeling, G. Capeling; W. J. Capeling; C. Castle; L. Castle; M. Darton; P. E. Dines; F. Ditton; W. Freed; W. Fullager; W. W. Fuller; E. Gamble; V. J. Gilbert; A. J. Gower, G. W. Green; R. Hall; J. Hanson; F. W. Harris; W. C. Harris; C Hart; T. Herd; A. A. Hills; S. Hopper; R. Hyland, W. Jackson; W. Knott; T. Lancefield; E. Luckhurst; H. D. Marshall; A. Martin; F. A. Millen; C. Nicholls; C. H. W. Norman; H. Oliver; S Oliver; P Orpin; A. W. Paine; H Paine; W. T. Paine; A Potter; A. Priddle; W. Reeves; E. E. Ridley; W. Scott; H. Sidney; J. Silverwood; B. Smith; H. C. Stent; A. Tanton; C. E. Tomlin; G. T. Trowell; J. West; W. G. Wheeler; A. A. Wood; F. J. Wood; E. J. Woolley; H. Woolley; E. E. Young.

KENT 12, MAIDSTONE, was raised by Mrs. Wood Martyn and registered in 1910. By arrangement with the Committee of the West Kent General Hospital a short course in the wards of this hospital has been a part of the annual training of the members.

The detachment was mobilised on October 14th, 1914, and the Howard de Walden Institute with accommodation for thirty beds was completely prepared to receive patients in less than two hours.

The support received has been of great value, contributions having been most generously forthcoming. Four trained nurses have given their services without any remuneration. The Commandant is Joint Assistant County Director for the 3rd Division of the county, and undertakes the distribution of the wounded when station convoys arrive.

Commandant and Medical Officer—Dr. F. T. Travers.
Lady Superintendent—Miss Burfield.
Quartermaster—Miss Mercer.

Members.—Ruth E. Bensted ; Florence Betts ; Gladys Boorman ; Dorothy Cadman ; Hilda Cadman ; Joan Campbell-Bannerman ; Gladys Clifford ; Dorothy Cornwallis ; Louie M. Cowley ; Lady Nina Hughes D'Aeth ; Sylph Davey ; Ella Foord ; Kathleen Hills ; Nora Hoar ; K May Hughes ; Margaret Ley ; Magdalen Littlewood , Winifred Mercer , Grace Nickalls ; Maud Nickalls ; Mary Scott ; Peggy Scott ; Flora Walter ; Dorothy Whitehead ; Katherine Wintour ; Agnes Warner.

Kent 13, Cranbrook, has charge of the transport for this section of the county and is doing useful practical work. The Ashford section has helped with orderly duty in conjunction with Kent 11.

Commandant—Captain Torkington.
Medical Officer—Dr. C. Brett.
Quartermaster—W. Lewis.
Pharmacist—A. Hudson.

Section Leaders—E. Fever , H Parker.

Members—F Bookin , F. Burchett ; E. Burnham ; G. Coleman , F. Craddock , W. Craddock ; A. Darton ; D. Fox , F.

Fryer, G. Fuggle; H. S. Gaudy; E. Gibson; F. Goldsmith, G. Goodman; E. Greenstreet; G. Henneker; E. Hewison; R. Horne; G. Jenner; W. S. Jordan; E. W. King; A Marshall, H. Muchell; S. Nash; W. N. Neve; E. Penfold, H. A. Rosson; E. Rumens; J. Sharp; F. E. Stanley; R. Swinard; E R. Tasman; W. H. Trimlett, A. Tye; J. Waters; F. Worsley.

Members who have enlisted —H. Alexander; H. Baker; S. Beeken; G. Gasden; T. Luck; G. Palmer; C Parks; F. Philpott; R. Sanders.

KENT 13 (*attached*), TONBRIDGE TOWN " Bearers Squad," was registered as a men's detachment in the autumn of 1914. The men have since that time been engaged in transport and orderly duties at the Tonbridge V.A.D. Hospital. Local medical men have freely given their services in the training of the members.

Commandant—CECIL CROFTS.
Medical Officer—DR. J. MANNING WATTS.
Quartermaster—MR. B. GABRIEL.

Members —A. W. Ablethorpe; F. H. Abley; E. Bishop; H. Burson; W. A. Carling; A W. Coburn; A E. Cornell, J. S. Cottle; C. H. Crofts; W. J. Duval; R. East; G. Faircloth; A. E. Featherstone, T. Fulcher; A. Gutsell; P. Hamblin; C. Harvey; L. Hazell, C. Horner, J. E Langdon-Davies; J. Long; T. C. Love; W. Mackay; F. Mockford; E. Morley; W. Neal; W. G. Neve; F. Packman, C. H. Page; J. Payne; R. H. Pottinger; B. W. Reecks; A. Ross; F. Small; J. Spillett; E. A. Stevens; W. K. Storr; T. Treen; B. E. Tye, A. S. Waghorn; T. W. Young.

KENT 14, MAIDSTONE, was enrolled in 1910. Soon after the outbreak of war Hayle Place, lent by Lord Romney, with accommodation for seventy patients, was fully equipped.

On October 14th, 1914, fifty-three wounded Belgians arrived; and, in all, 400 patients, of whom 100 were Belgians, have been treated.

The expenses of the hospital are certified by a Finance Committee with Mr. George Marsham as chairman. The hospital is most fortunate in having many willing workers outside the detachment.

Mr. J. Pickard has organised a band of men who act as transport bearers and orderlies, and Mr. Bernard Haynes has charge of the arduous work of arranging transport. Dr. Jones helps the Medical Officer and the Rev. E. Hardcastle is Chaplain. Mrs. Lilley is in charge of the kitchen; Mrs. Falwasser and Mrs. Whitton are the sisters in charge of the wards.

Commandant—MRS. WILSON-SMITH.
Medical Officer—DR. GROUND.
Lady Superintendent—MISS A. SAUNDERS.
Quartermaster—MISS K. WEEKS.

Members—Mabel Balston, Margaret Bridge; Aline Cholmeley; Mabel Cornwallis, Yvonne Cornwallis, Maud Harrison, Phyllis Hartridge; Minnie Killick, Cecily Kennard; Henrietta Keays-Young, Julia Keays-Young, Jessie Marsham, Constance Marsham; Mollie Marsham; Amy Pope, Annie Roberts; Mary E Reatchlons, Mary Reatch-lons, Zoe Roe, Eleanor Ruck; Honble Ruth Scarlett; Laura de Visme Thomas, Ella de Visme Thomas, Dorothy

Thomas; Edith Tronsdell; Evelyn Tronsdell; Louisa Warde; Dorothy Warde; Gladys Warde; Laura Wigan; Harriet Wigan; Grace Young.

KENT 15, BROMLEY. This detachment was formed as a St. John Ambulance Company prior to the organisation of the county V.A.D., and transferred to the county organisation on its inception.

On the declaration of war thirty of its members joined the regular forces. Railway employees of the detachment have been debarred from active participation by reason of diminished staff, the balance of the detachment, Chislehurst in particular, is serving with V.A.D. Hospitals.

Commandant—T. HEALEY.
Quartermaster—W. E. CLIFFORD.

No. 1.—ST. LUKE'S SECTION.—*Joined H.M. Forces.*—G. T. Attle; G. Barnett; H. Billinge; J. Bloomfield; H. B. Burden; S. Bush; A. C. Brouard; W. Collins; C. E Farrow; F. Field; W. J. Field; W. S. Graty; J. W. Hubbard; H. W. Johnson; C. F. Mumford; A. P. Padgham; H. J. Yeates, and Sergt. Field.

Employed locally.—T. H. Barnard; J. Field; M. Horlock; W. Stevens.

No. 2—CENTRAL HALL SECTION.—*Joined H.M. Forces.*—A. Brown; H. D. Burden; A. E. Burford; S. Craker; E. Hawkins; W. N. Hobday; T. Stone, C Waters.

Employed locally.—E. G. Follett; H. S. Harden; C. Hobbs; J. Huckle; J. E. Napier; R. J. Orgles; S. Pinneger.

No. 3.—CHISLEHURST SECTION.—*Joined H.M. Forces.*—F. Rouse; B. Streatfield.

Employed locally.—W. Aley; T. Barber (Jr.); T Barber; W. Beckington; A. Bone, F. Dixon; W. Fellis; H. Head; H. Humphrey; H. Lawrence; H. Pinyon; M. Taylor, H. White; T. White; C. Wood.

No. 4.—Orpington Section.—*Joined H.M. Forces.*—S. W. Conway ; A. Geary ; E. J. Patterson ; A. Skinner.

Employed locally.—W. Bridgeman ; T. W. Burgess ; R. Gainsford ; B. Goodyer ; E. Jennings ; W. Lane ; W. Newman ; J. Samson ; H. Tomlinson ; W. Wood.

Kent 16, Gravesend, was first organised in 1910, and owed its existence to the energy of Mrs. Bruce-Culver, its first Quartermaster. The present Medical Officer was first Commandant, and his lectures have been of great benefit in the training of the members.

Kent 16 in conjunction with Kent 92 have prepared and are now working at three hospitals :—

(1) Parish Room, All Hallows ; lent by Rev. R. Hammond, where over seventy cases have been treated. Sister-in-charge, Miss M. Grenfell-Hill, R.R.C.

(2) Meadow Room, Cobham, accommodation for nineteen cases ; lent by the Misses Stevens, and prepared by them and a number of ladies from the neighbourhood. About eighty patients have already been admitted. Sister-in-charge, Miss Ethel Swinton (sister of the well-known " Eye-Witness ").

(3) The Yacht Club, Gravesend, under Kent 92.

The Hospitals at All Hallows and Gravesend are financially controlled by an Executive Committee, of which Colonel Sir Gilbert Parker is Chairman.

Lord Darnley presides over the Cobham Hospital Committee.

Commandant—Miss Agnes O. Caswell.
Medical Officer—Dr. C. Dismorr.
Lady Superintendent—Miss Isabella Rosher.
Quartermaster—Miss E. Tansley.

Members.—Maud Armstrong; Florence August; Mary Bathurst ; Margaret Beer ; Emily Blake ; Hattie Claret, Cicely Clark ; Hilda Crook; Marjorie Davey; Christine Donaldson ; Beatrice Dyble ; Elsie Gates , Frances Green ; Grace Harris ; Audrey Hayes ; Evaline Hooper-Smith ; Hilda Huggins ; Grace Jones ; Amy King ; Maud King ; Marjorie Lund , Ada Marsh ; Mildred Newcombe ; Catherine Posgate ; Dorothy Poynter ; Kate Reeves ; Florence Rowe ; Edith Sackett ; Ellen Scratton ; Hilda Shaw , Lucy Shaw ; Bessie Shields ; Winnie Shields ; Gertrude Shuttlewood ; Helen Shuttlewood ; Alice Smith ; Olive Tanner ; Dorothy Thompson ; Maud Thompson ; Sophie Thompson ; Janet Waldegrave ; Winifred Winnett ; Gladys Wood ; Grace Wood.

Kent 17, Walmer. Surgeon-General F. H. Benson was asked by Lady George Hamilton in 1911 to raise a men's detachment in conjunction with Kent 22, and lectures were given by him.

On General Benson being appointed Assistant County Director, Dr. Mason, Medical Officer for Kent 22, assisted him to form a detachment.

In 1913 the command was taken over by Dr. H. Harrison, who had already given valuable assistance. On the outbreak of war Dr. Harrison was compelled to take on other work and had to resign, although he kindly continued as Medical

Officer. The present Commandant then took charge of the detachment, which is fully prepared for any work which may be assigned to it.

Commandant—CHAS. R. TAYLOR.
Medical Officer—DR. H. HARRISON.
Quartermaster—T. BAXTER.

Members.—J. H. Atkins ; A. R. Betts ; C. S Bignold ; J. J. Bingham ; B. Bradshaw ; C. Capp ; F. Denham ; W. G Dunn ; C. Fieldsend ; A. French ; A. Graves ; W. Honey ; E. Hunt , E. C. Lewis ; J. G Newing ; W. Norris ; L. Petts , P J. Rayworth , H. M. Romney ; T Sneller ; R. Stylo ; E Thomas ; J. Waller ; G. Wellard ; L. V. West ; H. T. Williams ; W. Williams.

KENT 17 (*attached*), TENTERDEN, owed its inception to the splendid efforts of Mr. H. Ker, who was Assistant County Director, 5th Division, Kent, until taking up a commission in the regular army. The detachment has supplied night orderlies, regularly since mobilisation, to the Tenterden and Rolvenden Hospitals. Five stretchers have been presented to the detachment.

Commandant—L. H. BROWNING.
Quartermaster—J. BACKSHALL.

Members —C. A. Adams ; E Ballard , A Barrington , A Bennett , F Bennett , A Bourne ; H Bourne , C Brown , F Burden ; W. Chitt , C Corke , G. Curteis ; W Dapson , G Edmonds , B Grake , A Hilder , A Holmes , F Holdstock , C Jarvis ; L Maynard , H McCarter ; — McLeod , S. J Sharpe , W Sharpe , N Tickner , — Tickner ; A Wallis ; G Waterman , M White , S N Willson

KENT 17 (*attached*), STONE, has undertaken, with every success, the ambulance and all similar work

in connection with the big military hospital at
Ingress Abbey.

Commandant—E. D. CARRICK.
Medical Officer—DR. STANLEY.
Pharmacist—E. J. COX.
Quartermaster—F. T. EBERHARDT.

Section Leaders.—G. Barnes; H. Bartrum; W. Germaney;
H. Williams.

Members.—F. Acland; J. G. Adams; F. Austin; H C. Barnes;
B T. Beaumont; D. Boorman; C. W. Bullock; D. Busby;
C. Coker; S. Coker; J. Colven; H A. Coulter; A. Eber-
hardt; W. Eberhardt; R. Entwistle; J. French; R.
Gray; A. Green; R. Hayes; E. Haywood; A. Hodges;
R. James; J. Jennison; A. E. Kent; H. Lane; W. Line-
ham, G. Livingstone; F. Masters; F. Montgomery; F.
Munn; A. Nettlingham; J. Pink; A. Reid; P. Sanders;
A. Saunders; J. Shoard; G. Smith; W. Sparrow; B.
Steadman; S. Vickery; W. Watson; J. Webster.

KENT 17 (*attached*), BEXLEY, owes its genesis
to the initiative of a committee presided over by
Sir Guildford Molesworth, the details being worked
out by Mr. G. P. Baker and Mr. J. Cutcliffe,
assisted by Dr. T. Hinds. Enrolment took place
on September 7th, 1914, and a course of lectures
was given by Dr. Hinds and practices held with
most satisfactory results. The detachment was
mobilised on October 14th, and thanks to the
generosity of the inhabitants of Bexley the men
have been assisted in the purchase of uniforms.
The Bexley Brewery Co. have kindly lent one of

their vans, which has been fitted up as an ambulance wagon, while ground for practice has been generously placed at the detachment's disposal by Mr. Ford and Mrs. Burridge. Useful work is being carried on regularly.

Commandant—COL. RADFORD.
Medical Officer—DR. T. W. HINDS.
Quartermaster—MR. A. COVILL.
Pharmacist—MR. LEADBETTER.
Class Secretary—MR. CHRISTOPHERSON.

Section Leaders.—W. J. Evans; F. Hurdle; W. Porter; C. Vessey.

Members.—G. P. Baker; T. N. Cannon; N. Christopherson; W. Chuter; E. Crick; J. Cutcliffe; H. Edwards; C. Garrett; E. G. Harvey; J. F. Harvey; N. Hudson; A. W. James; J. W. Judd; G. T. Lawrence; S. Leadbetter; A. Lincoln; C. W. Mann; R. Marshall; T. E. Parker; J. Pitt; J. Reid; J. Rendell; E. H. Russell; H. Slade; H. Smith; H. J. Standley; W. J. Taylor; H. A Turner; F. Wheeler.

KENT 17 (*attached*), HAWKHURST. The members have done thoroughly useful work as night orderlies at the Lillesden Hospital and have assisted at all times in the transport of wounded to and from the station and Central Military Hospital.

Commandant—A. C. MOORE.
Medical Officer—DR. ROBERT EDWARDS.
Quartermaster—SYDNEY NEWMAN.

Members—J. T. E Davis; C. Giles; E. Hardcastle; A. Harrison; V Hutchinson; H. Hyder; P. Jenner; G. Martin; J. Mennie; F. Reed; J. Suter; G. Sivyer; W. Sivyer; W. Wilmot.

H

KENT 18, PEMBURY, formed in 1910 under Dr. Aldous, has worked continuously to make itself efficient, and in 1914 the Guardians of the Tonbridge Union allowed the members to nurse in their infirmary.

On October 14th, 1914, the order to mobilise was received, and in a very short time, thanks to the excellent arrangements made beforehand by the Quartermaster, the village Hall at Paddock Wood was converted into a hospital ready to receive twenty patients. After two months it was found necessary to transfer the hospital to the Church Institute, Pembury, lent by the Committee. Most generous gifts have been received, and car owners have willingly lent their motors for transport.

Fifty patients have been successfully treated, and no effort has been spared on the part of the Medical Officers, Drs. Storr, Simpson, Bradford, Mills, and Seely. The former Commandant was Dr. Crawford, who was Joint County Director for No. 3 Division, and had charge of the distribution of wounded when convoys arrived for the Tunbridge Wells group of hospitals. He accepted a commission in His Majesty's Forces in April, 1915.

Commandant—MRS. DOUGLAS WATSON.
Hon. Commandant—DR. CRAWFORD.
Medical Officer—DR. W. T. STORR.
Lady Superintendent—MISS ROBB.
Quartermaster—MISS HAINES.

Members.—Dorothy Andrews ; Phyllis Baker ; Sylvia Baker ; Joan Cartwright ; Phillis Crawford ; Janet Goffe ; Amy Herepath ; Fanny Kempster ; Marion Lambert ; Gemma Lees ; Annie Luck ; Kittie Luck ; Dora Molesworth ; Margery Mewburn ; Olive Mewburn ; Joyce Mewburn ; Marie Philpott ; Anna Perkin ; Dorothy Perkin ; Esther Perryman ; Ellen Pattison ; Mary Podmore ; Alice Simpson ; Kate Simpson ; Ethel Simpson ; Selina Storr ; Amy Storr ; May Storr ; Freda Storr ; Ada Terry ; Edith Hay Watson ; Sibyl Watson ; Brenda Watson ; Edith Wimshurst ; Edythe Whelan ; Florence Young.

KENT 18 (*attached*), EAST MALLING. Soon after the outbreak of war Mr. C. Baxendale offered to convert a wing of his residence, Clare House, into a hospital. Some alterations were made and a small but serviceable hospital, with two wards for seventeen men, was created. The equipment was lent by residents, and the linen and other necessaries by the Red Cross Society. Mr. Baxendale assumed responsibility for the finance, but invited the residents to assist, which suggestion was liberally responded to. The ladies of East Malling having previously organised a V.A. detachment, an efficient staff was ready for the opening of the hospital. The wards have been kept fairly full since the first convoy was received.

Commandant—SIR W. D. WILSON.

Medical Officer—DR. PARR DUDLEY.

Quartermaster—LADY DEANE WILSON.

Members—Lucy Ambler ; Gertrude Biggs, Florence Edith Bird ; Lily Blunden, Florence Blunden, Elizabeth Blunden ; Ada Buckland, Ethel Buckland ; Phyllis Buckland ; Owens Busbridge ; Mavis Busbridge ; Kate Lily Colegate ; Molly Dever-son ; Charlotte Downs ; Ethel May Elphic ; Bessie Godden ; Fanny Holder ; Florence Holder ; Phœbe Huggett ; Lydia Jenner ; Elizabeth Parr-Dudley ; Agnes Peppercorn ; Florence Peppercorn ; Hilda Silverston ; Isabel Smyth ; Henrietta Maria White ; Doris Wilson.

KENT 19, BOUGHTON, was formed in 1913.

Since the outbreak of war seventeen members have enlisted. The detachment is well prepared to undertake any duties assigned to it.

Commandant and Medical Officer—DR. H. WONNACOTT.
Quartermaster—C. W. SMITH.

Members.—A. I. W. Bones ; J. W. Bones ; W. P. Branchett ; L. H. Chambers ; M. E. Eades ; S. R. Fox ; J. Hayward ; R. J. Hopkins ; F. S. Horn ; H. Iddenten ; W. F. Miles ; R. H. Owen ; G. Packman ; R. Rooke ; H. Rooke ; W. A. Smith ; A. W. Spicer : A. E. Tong ; E. V. Turner ; W. A. Turner ; E. C. Wills ; A. Wood.

KENT 20, TENTERDEN, was started at Tenterden by Mrs. Peel at the request of Lady Cranbrook in 1911. The members of the detachment, at first under Dr. Skinner as Commandant, have been continuously preparing themselves for any emergency. When mobilised in October, 1914, the detachment sent reliefs to a local hospital until November, when a Red Cross Hospital was opened with sixteen beds. This was furnished to a great extent by the local residents, who were also most generous in sending contributions.

On November 30th, 1914, the first party of Belgian soldiers, fifteen in number, arrived.

Commandant—Miss CICELY PEEL.
Medical Officer—DR. DRING.
Quartermaster—Miss V. MILNE.

Members.—Dorothy Baker; Bertha Body; Gertrude Browning, Alice Collins; Marjorie Johnson; Gladys Johnstone; Ada Latter; Kate Love; Evelyn Mace; Dora Peel; Esther Peel; Edith Pinyon; Kathleen Pritchard; Blanche Pritchard; Helen Pritchard; Esther Pritchard; Edith Skelding; Christina Ticehurst; Kate Winser.

KENT 20 (*attached*), CHARING. This hospital was opened on October 14th, at the Parish Hall, lent by the Charing Parish Council. Local residents contributed liberally in money and equipment. The detachment had previously prepared themselves for the duties of a hospital by classes and practices, and are doing important work most capably.

Commandant and Medical Officer—
DR. LITTLEDALE.
Lady Superintendent—Miss FLORENCE ROTHERHAM.
Quartermaster—Mrs. LITTLEDALE.

Members—Ethel Ashwell; Hilda Beard; E. Mildred Fotheringham; Dorothy Hardwick; Evelyn Hardwick; Hilda Hardwick; Ethel Hickman, Louise Hickman; Fanny Hyland, Letitia Jennings; M Langford; H E. Littledale; Violet Littledale; Marjorie Machin; Daisy Mummery; Katharine Norwood, Alice Norwood, Lottie Reeves; Ethel Ross-Barker, Katharine Sayer; Helen Starey, Mary Starey, Agatha Sulston; Edith Swan; Margaret Swan; Mary Swan Molly White.

KENT 21, WESTERHAM, was formed in 1913, the initial effort being due to Miss Watney.

The detachment was mobilised in October, 1914, about twenty men being available. These acted as orderlies for the Dunsdale Hospital until Christmas, when an arrangement was made with a field ambulance, stationed in the locality, whereby this body took over the duties temporarily. Kent 21 has, since April, 1915, resumed this important work.

Commandant—G. N. WATNEY.
Medical Officer—J. R. RUSSELL.
Quartermaster—REV. C. A. STUBBS.

Members.—F. N Ashby; S. A. Bridgland; B. Brown; D. Brown; C. Chapman; W. N. Darkin; E. J. Drapper; C. R. Evans; A. Friend; A. Galloway; J. Gardner; A. Gingell; J. Greenlees; T. Greenlees; J. Haslett; P. Ingram; E. Jenner; E. Longley; P. May; F. H. Nellen; H. D. Pennicard; F. Shorter; J. Steven; W. G. Sweatman.

KENT 22, DEAL, was formed in 1912, with Dr. A. Mason, Miss Sandford, and Mrs. Wheeler as officers. Work went steadily on with lectures, drill, field work, etc. In 1913 Lady Sargant became Commandant, Dr. Mason remaining as Medical Officer; Mrs. Wheeler resigned, Miss D. M. Lapage replacing her. Lady Sargant was unable to continue the duties and became Hon. Commandant, Miss Sandford taking up her work, Miss E. M. Higginson becoming Lady Superintendent. The detachment gained much practical experience at the camps at Herne and Rolvenden. Lectures were given by doctors of Deal, notably by Dr. Mason, Dr. Ward, Fleet-Surgeon R. Hill and Dr. White, and each member in turn received a fortnight's hospital training at the Victoria Hospital. During the war two members at a time have been working at the Royal Marine Infirmary.

On the outbreak of war St. Anselm's, Walmer, a former residence of Mr. Justice and Lady Sargant, was fitted up as a hospital, the people of Deal and Walmer contributing generously. On Kent 142 being formed Miss Lapage transferred to that detachment, Miss C. M. Reid replacing her.

Lady George Hamilton allowed Deal Castle to be used as a store and gave much assistance.

On October 14th, 1914, mobilisation took place and Belgian wounded were quickly installed. Two hundred and fifty patients in all have kept the beds fully occupied.

Owing to domestic trouble Miss Sandford was compelled to resign, and Lady Sargant returned to her former post. Miss Higginson went to work with the French Red Cross and Mrs. Lloyd, Lady Superintendent of Kent 142, acted during her absence.

Kitchen arrangements are admirably carried out

by Miss Bowman, and the residents of St. Margaret's have been most generous.

Commandant—LADY SARGANT.
Lady Superintendent—MISS HIGGINSON.
Medical Officer—DR. MASON.
Quartermaster—MISS C. M. REID.

Members.—Iola Baynes; Eileen Boothby; Alice Bowman; Sylvia Bushe; Doreen Cavanagh; Eleanor Cottew; Emmeline Darwall; Mabel Denne; Holly Fisher; Evelyn Gardner; Audrey Jackson; Phyllis Jackson; Sydney Jackson; Olive Lapage; Winifred Lapage; Eleanor Macrae; Dorothy Matthews; Ada McCann; Hilda Mills; Adela Monins; Dorothy Morse; Marjory Morse; Phyllis Ryder Richardson; Enid Schón; Ursula Schon; Rosamund Smythe; Enid Thomas; Dora Thomson; Elsie Thomson.

KENT 22 (*attached*), MARGATE.   Full details of this detachment's work are given under Kent 152.

Medical Officer—DR. THOMSON.
Lady Superintendent—MISS ANNE CHAPMAN.
Quartermaster—MISS ETHEL JAMES.

KENT 22 (*attached*), BIRCHINGTON, had no detachment at the outbreak of war, but when Dr. Garfield Williams inspected Thanet he realised the possibilities of this bracing town. He enlisted the services of the principal officials, including doctors, Commandant and trained nurses, and accepted the use of a Red Cross office lent by Mr. and Mrs. Harvey.

Certificated candidates came forward and attended lectures, had practical experience at the hospitals, and by October a detachment of thirty-eight members was ready. Mrs. Willett lent a store in the village for equipment, and at Quex Park two large motors were fitted with ambulance bodies (these have been since used for the whole of Thanet).

On mobilisation Mansford House, a Unitarian convalescent home (kindly lent to the detachment) was quickly prepared and Belgian wounded were installed.

St. Mary's Home also took in a number and worked under the detachment for a month, until Quex Park, the home of Major and Mrs. Powell-Cotton, which had been lent temporarily to the Westgate detachment, was free.

Under Mrs. Holmes as Matron at Quex Park, and Miss Worthington at Mansford House, the staff has worked steadfastly and well.

Commandant—MRS. H. B. POWELL-COTTON.
Medical Officer—DR. WORTHINGTON.
Lady Superintendents—
MISS WORTHINGTON AND MRS. HOLMES.
Quartermaster—MRS. HAROLD COBB.

Members.—Dorothy Elspeth de Vosta Andraade ; Mary Blackhurst ; Clara Lasey Buss, Marjorie Tylden Buss ; Alice Cobb, Edith Mary Cossey, Janet Dallin, Minnie Dawes ; Maud Elinor Harris, Mary Holmes ; Alice Keeley ; Florence Perfect, Emily Reeves, Phyllis Roberts, Elsie Alice Smith ; Hilda Stone ; Lucy Stone ; Mildred Swinford ; Dora Evelyn Watson ; Fanny Maud Watson ; Charlotte Wilhelmina Worthington ; Elizabeth Mary Worthington.

KENT 23, SHEERNESS-ON-SEA, at first constituted part of Kent 41, but in 1913 was formed as
a separate detachment for Sheerness. The members have taken part in several field days, and the
drills have been well attended. There being no
hospital in the town the men have no regular
duties, but deal with all cases of emergency. A
depôt for the receipt of garments has been opened.
The Commandant, Mr. F. H. Watson, is on active
service.

Acting Commandant and Medical Officer.
DR. L. A. WINTER.

Quartermaster—MR. H. RAYNER CATT.

Members.—T. G Allen ; F. W. Bickel ; O. V. Boakes ; R. V.
Borner ; C. E. Bowden ; W. A. Broad ; E. J. Castle ; R.
Carvalho ; A. J. Davis ; F. Day ; W. J. Freeman ; A. G.
French ; S A. Hadlow ; W. H. Kingdon ; G. W. Lochhead ;
W. H. Maples ; E. A. Monday ; A. Nightingale ; J. L.
Nethercoat ; G. W. Pack ; E E. Pankhurst ; E. G. Pear-
son , G. J Peed ; W. H. B. Quick ; E. J. Ratcliff ; A. O.
Reece ; G. J. Rogers ; J Rogers , C. F. Saddleton ; F. G.
Saunders ; W. Saunders ; C. A. Snelling ; W. A. Southgate ;
E. J. Stride ; D. Stride ; H. L. Sutton ; G. Swift ; G.
Thomas ; W. Thomas , C. F. Woodcock.

KENT 24, FOLKESTONE, was formed in 1910, and
has charge of the Manor House Hospital at Folkestone, one of the largest of Kent's voluntary
hospitals, and has been doing splendid work from
the outset of hostilities.

Commandant—HONOURABLE FLORENCE DALY.

Members.—Dorothy Beaney ; Jennie Boyd ; Kate Brenchley ;
Katharine Chevalier ; Lena Curzon-Smith ; Mabel Eastes ;

Emma Eiffe; Amelia Fantham; Mary Fitzgerald; Minnie Fowler; Louisa Hibbard; Florence Hill; M. M. Lucas; Florence Millgate; Adelaide Moore; Ada Orton; Florence Palmer; Lilian Penn, Edith Pilcher; Kathleen Reid; May Rowlands; Lucy Shillingford; Alice Stocker; Florence Strood; Maud Wood.

KENT 25, TUNBRIDGE WELLS, was formed at the outbreak of war from the division of the St. John Ambulance Brigade. A men's first aid class was organised, and 120 men attended, of whom thirty-six ultimately joined the brigade.

A liberal response was made by the public to an appeal for funds to provide uniforms, and the men are now equipped in khaki.

Three new stretchers have also been presented. The Quartermaster and ten men are on active service. The transport for Tunbridge Wells and Tonbridge group of the Chatham section of Kent is conducted by Mr. W. L. Bradley of Tonbridge, with the assistance of the Commandant and Mr. Cecil Crofts, the distribution of the patients being conducted by Dr. Watson.

Commandant and Medical Officer—DR. DYER.
Quartermaster—LIEUT E. R. HICKMOTT.

Members—H Albrow; W. Avard; C. Barefield; H. Bone; L Claydon; T Coombes, W. E. Cunningham, S. W. Dawes, W Dibby, — Faircloth, S Faithfull, H G Foote; J W Goodwin, A T Goodyear, A E Hallett, P Hammond, S W Harmer, W J F Harmer; J. Hayes, J. Hayward, T. Hayward, W B Hemsley, R Howlett; C. Hicks, A Hobbs; H Honess, A. Jury, J. Kempster;

T. C. Knight; T. Lester; A. W. Luxton; F. W. Mason; S. H. Muffett; W. F. Muffett; J. Neeve; P. Noakes; O. Norman; G. Nuth; J. C. Nuth; G. Peskett; C. Reader; H. Saxby; L. Scott; G. Spurrell; W. Stanford; G. Stovens; H. A. Stonham; T. Showler; W. Vaughan; A. C. Watts; H. G. Whitby; H. White; H. M. Wise; H. Woodcock; C. Young.

KENT 26, FOLKESTONE, was brought into being in 1911, and the members have met continuously for lectures and practices.

At mobilisation the members were called to the Imperial Hotel, Hythe, which had been commandeered for the reception of a large number of wounded Belgian soldiers. The hotel was cleared three days later, and since October 21st Kent 26, with Kent 24, have together been working at the Manor House. This hospital has one hundred beds. It is situated on the Leas, overlooking the sea.

Gifts of all kinds have been received from very many kind donors.

The two detachments have also had charge of a small dressing station in one of the " soldiers' clubs " at Shorncliffe camp, and a member attends daily to dress injuries amongst the soldiers.

Commandant—MRS. MOULE.
Medical Officer—DR. GORE.
Quartermaster—MISS L. FITZGERALD.

Members.—Mary Ambler; Florence Andries; Madeleine Andries; Martho Andries; Josephine Baker; Mrs. Carpenter;

Kathleen Cornes; Dorothy D'Armes; May Davis; Elsie Deck; May Francis; Mary Golden; Jenny Hills; Elsie Hopper; Annette Irving; Hilda Jervis; Sybil Lawson; Elizabeth McCliment; Edith Mempes; Kathleen Moule; Eliza Poston; Winifred Shillingford; Olive Shipp; Barbara Simms, Emily West; Grace Wood.

KENT 28, ROLVENDEN, was organised in 1911.

Regular drills and lectures were held, and the British Red Cross Camp for Kent for 1914 was held at Rolvenden on a site lent by Mr. F. Coombe Baker. Two hundred and thirty members were present from all parts; the camp was of especial help, as it was struck only ten days before war broke out.

The detachment is drawn principally from the village of Rolvenden, and, when mobilised, proved fully equal to the emergency; the hospital, which was a bare parish room, being in a very short time a charming little ward ready to receive twenty patients.

Commandant—MRS. COOMBE BAKER.
Medical Officer—DR. P. C. COLLS.
Lady Superintendent—MISS K. BISHOP.
Quartermaster—MRS. SMITH-MARRIOTT.
Assist. Quartermaster—MISS ETHEL PARKER.

Members.—Mary Barker; Rhoda Becken; Sarah Brown; Emily Burden; Jennie Burden; Hetty Burden; Edith Button; A. Cook; Dorothy Guest; Grace Herring; Mary Hinds; Annie Mann; Pattie Piper; Fanny Poile; Olive Southon; Cissy Swaffer; Kate Swinyard; May Terry; Katherine Tweedie; Laura Tweedie; May Weston; Harriet Wood; Carrie Woodwards.

Night Orderlies.—G. Ballam ; J Becken ; A. Blackman ; A. Bourne ; C. Brown ; R. Burden ; B. Burden ; F. Burden ; G. Carpenter ; A. Cook ; A. Fright ; F. Geerings ; F. Judge ; E. Killick ; L. Maynard ; J. Parker ; F. Russell ; W. Sharp ; C. Smith ; H. Swaffer.

KENT 29, MARGATE. At the outbreak of war a meeting was called to form a V.A.D. men's detachment. Some eighty men (since increased) gave in their names as voluntary helpers. Classes were formed, with Dr. B. Richards as lecturer, stretcher drill exercises being also carried out under Captain Turner.

Detachments 29 and 31 were thus created from these volunteers. The Margate Ambulance Corps joined the detachments and placed all their appliances at the disposal of the Commandants. Since mobilisation—on October 13th, 1914—both detachments have assisted at the transport of six hundred wounded soldiers. The members have also carried out very arduous duties as orderlies.

Several friends have given stretchers and carrying-sheets ; motor-cars and ambulances have been generously placed at the disposal of the transport officer.

The two detachments jointly undertake all the work carried out.

The transport arrangements are in the hands of Hon. Commandant D. T. Milne (assisted by W. E. Enderby, until the latter was accepted for work in France). A large amount of preliminary organisation fell to the lot of Mr. Milne; Assistant-Quartermaster Mr. G. A. Watson has undertaken all secretarial duties of both detachments since mobilisation.

Commandant—B. J. GARRAWAY.
Medical Officer—DR. R. THOMSON.
Quartermaster—W. MILLS.

Section Leaders.—W. J. Hecker and W. J. Munns.

Members.—E. Amos; J. R. Amos; A. W. Barry, A. D. Bettles; P. M Brophy; S H Brown; O. J. Baldwin; F. C. Cobb; T. Coleman; A. W. Elkin, E J. Furborough; G. A Foster; F. S. Gahan; F. T. Gahan; A. F. Hewer; E. E Levitt; W. H. Linnell; B. Lowery; G. J. Mahoney; J. Matthews; L. G. Matthews; H. V. Mitchell; J. Peachey; E. Richmond, R. H. Roberts; A. J. Swain; J. W. Sadd; J. G. Sayer; F. J. Sayer; H. D. Tappenden; J. T. Tatham; J. C. Tayler; H. M. Wainman; H. Walker-Smith; G. L. Watson; T. G. Webb.

KENT 30, SANDGATE, has charge, with other detachments, of the Bevan Home, Sandgate, Kent's largest voluntary hospital. The home is very pleasantly situated near the sea, and has, with its annexe Devonshire House, 250 beds, twenty-five of which are reserved for officers. The hospital was opened on October 8th, 1914, and has received to date 1995 patients, 310 of whom have been Belgians. The members have shown what voluntary effort can achieve when the workers have plenty of energy and adaptability and have their hearts in what they are doing. The detachment came into being in 1910.

Commandant—SISTER MILLIE MUMFORD.
Medical Officer—DR. J. E. CALVERLEY.
Lady Superintendent—MRS. MAYNE.
Quartermaster—MRS. CHAMBERS.

(See list of members under Kent 36.)

KENT 31, MARGATE (see Kent 29).
Commandant—J. W. WALTON.
Medical Officer—DR. GRAHAM STEWART.
Quartermaster—C. ENDERBY.
Pharmacist—W. H. MONK.

Section Leaders.—G. Enderby and F. Shaw.

Members—R. B. Amos ; R. J. Amos ; E. Ashby ; F. G. Brig-hurst ; A C. Bryant ; C. C. Burt ; P. J. Calcutt ; A. L. G. Campbell ; F. W. Coleman ; J. Combley ; W. Combley ; H. H. Davis ; E. M. Dungey ; J. Forbes ; C. W. G. Griffin ; T. Geary ; H. E. Hester ; E. J. Hobbs ; C. W. Hobbs ; E. W. Horn ; C. E. Jarman ; J. Jury ; W. G. Kemp ; S. H. Lamport ; A. E. Lovely ; J. A. Markey ; P. McCardle ; J. Olliver ; W. Ovens ; H. G. Philps ; R. C. Price ; J. Rattray ; R. Roscoe ; G. J. Shelley ; F. Stanley ; H. Tannenbaum ; R. W. Terrell ; J. M. Tillett.

KENT 32, CHERITON, was started in Cheriton five years ago.

At the outbreak of war, with the permission of the local authorities, the detachment got ready to open the Girls' School, Cheriton, as a hospital, but it was found that schools could not be used. The members therefore undertook to work at the Bevan Hospital, Sandgate, keeping their organisation intact, in case of emergency; and the mobilisation grant of £10 from the B.R.C.S. was handed over to that hospital.

Commandant—MRS. NEPEAN.
Medical Officer—DR. PRIDMORE.
Quartermaster—MISS MARIE JACQUES.

Members.—Lucy Bewsher; Violet Bloomfield; Marguerite Bourne; Marianne Burnett; — Butcher; Louise Childs, Florence Coleman; Lily Coveney; Emma Jane Dennis; Agnes Green; Isabella Hill; Lily Jacobs; Esther Miller; Jessie Miller; Althea Money; Marjorie Money; May Nicolas; Flora Pook, Doris Milligan; Jean Venner; Lily Venner; Dorothy Willis; Mabel Wilson.

KENT 33, BROMLEY, commenced work, at the declaration of war, under Quartermaster W. E. Clifford (of Kent 15). Dr. A. C. Haslam, the medical officer, gave a series of brilliant lectures on first aid, and as a result fifty-six members have been successful at subsequent examinations. On August 24th, 1914, the present Commandant was appointed, with Mr. Thomas Gayford as Quartermaster. The detachment was established on a sound basis, and the equipment and uniform fund started with a concert most kindly arranged by Mr. Priter. Other friends have generously assisted, and the detachment is now equipped with stretchers, water-bottles, haversacks, etc. Forty-five men are

I

uniformed. A rearrangement of the staff, consequent upon the Quartermaster's regretted enforced absence from Bromley, brought about the well-deserved promotion of Mr. Head. The order to mobilise found the detachment ready, and at midday on October 14th, 1914, the first convoy of wounded men was very successfully detrained at Bromley South Station. Work has been continuous since then, many ambulance trains having been unloaded at all hours. The detachment has had the distinction of having transferred nearly one-third of the sick and wounded received in Kent. Other duties have been carried out successfully, the most important being orderly work at the many hospitals. Beyond this, the members are perfecting themselves with nursing classes, drills and field schemes. Best thanks are due to Mr. Bert Harris, and to Mr. Jury, of the Pictorial Enterprises, Ltd., for entertainments given on behalf of the funds ; also to the trustees of St. Luke's Institute, the Trustees of the Wesleyan Church Hall, and many other friends. Gratitude to Miss Irene Wheeler Bennett is here expressed for her help with roller bandaging ; to Miss Winifred Mather for transport assistance ; to Dr. Haslam and Dr. Craster ; to Messrs. Pierson and Parke ; to Mr. C. W. Berry ; to Major and Mrs. Wilson of Eltham Court for loan of Wolseley Ambulance Car, and to the many other kind friends who have been so very willing to help the detachment. Mr. H. D. Reynolds was secretary until joining the colours in May, 1915.

Commandant—PAUL CRESWICK.
Honorary Commandant—H. G. HOSKIER.
Medical Officer—DR. A. C. HASLAM.
Quartermaster—F. E. HEAD.
Pharmacist—H. D. KELF.
Transport Control (Hon. Commandant Kent 54)—
P. H. ASHTON.

Section Leaders.—H. Gayford; M. Gray, L Harvey-Lowe, I. Humphrey; T. H. Jayes, G. H. Last; S. G. Nash, A. W. Stalam, F H. Sheriff

Members—E. R. Andrews, A Attwood; H. A. Balding; S. Belsey; F. Buckman; R Catterson; N. Clark; A. F. Collins; S H. Collins, J. H Covil, P S. Cox; R. Craker; R. Davey; W. Davis; G Day; A. Dickson, T T Eardley; W. Eglington; G. J. H. Forbes; W Fox; F Gardiner, T. Gayford; H. Godfrey, H. H Greenhill, W E. Gregory, R. Guthrie, R C Guthrie, L Gurney-Smith; J. H. Gurney-Smith; W H. Haigh, A Hains; A Harman; E Harman; L Harman; R. Hellyer; F. Herbert; A Hickmott; L H. Hillman, F E. Humble; C. H. Jenner; H Langrish, E J Lovell, J E Masters, A. C. Miles; S J. Miles, G. A Morris, G. H Morris, S T D Mortimer; N. Newcombe, N. F. Patten, A H Pockett; L C. Priest; H. A Randall, W E. Randall, E P Ripley; H D. Reynolds, T H Saunders; A P Sharland, J C. Shepherd, F Simmons, D. Strike; F. White, W. Willson.

Recruits—H Avery, W S Bibby, G Brown, W. Carpenter; D Cook, H Cook, H W Cook, F Craker, F Hartridge; — Hickman, A J Howe, — Kemp, — Kibble, E. W Lash; G. E. Lear; R. Longthorne, P Mitchell; F. W New; W. Pierson P. J Poindestie, R W Poindestie, — Saunders,

F. C. Smith; H. D. Smith; F. Stiff; — Theobald; F. H. Thorburn; F. G. Wilkins; E. A. Woodhall.

Deputy Transport Control.—R. Gilliard.
Instructor.—S. G. Nash.
Secretary.—F. H. Sheriff.

Note.—Very many of the above have temporarily joined His Majesty's forces.

Kent 34, Folkestone, was formed in 1911, and was maintained by weekly drills, instruction, and summer camps.

Owing to the unavoidable resignation of the Commandant, Mrs. Thornton Gilbert, the detachment was unable to organise a hospital, but joined Kent 30, Sandgate, and assisted in equipping the Bevan Home. By the efforts of the members money and equipment was collected.

When the detachment was mobilised on October 16th eighteen qualified members were working at the Bevan Home, together with a number of recruits, as probationers and ward maids. The work at the hospital has been continuous ever since mobilisation, and the majority of the members are now fully certificated.

Commandant and Quartermaster—Miss M. Peden.
Lady Superintendent—Miss L. Auty.

(List of Members given under Kent 36, Hythe.)

KENT 35, CANTERBURY, conducts all transport, supplies orderlies and male nurses for the Canterbury group of hospitals.

Commandant and Medical Officer—DR. FERGUSON.
Quartermaster—F. HOLGATE-SMITH.
Pharmacist—G. I. HOBBIS.

Members—W. Abrams; G. P Argrave; W. G. Barter; C. M. Bennett, D. Breeze; C. J. Brodie; R. B Brown; J. C Charrison; W. G. C Cheeseman; E Clark; J. B. Daniel, E. V. Dawe; C. C. Elam; J. Ellis; G. Goldfinch; P. L. Hall; S. Harding; J. I. Hargreaves; A. M. Hayward; C. Howes; J. E. Jarvis; L. Kemp; W. A. King; R. S. O. Lee; F. G. Link; H. F. W. Lyons; F. J. Mann; H. W. McConnell; W. F. R. Mist; A. Pearce; E. Pepper; R. P. Pettyfer; L. C. H. Sills; E C. Tomalin; S W. Vincett, F. J. Wells; A. A. Wicks; H E. Wicks; P. W. A. Wilson; F. Wood; J. H. Worsfold.

KENT 36, HYTHE, was organised in 1910 by Mrs. Congreve. In 1911 Mrs. Congreve, having left Hythe, the present Commandant took charge. At the outbreak of war all preparations were made to open a hospital, but at the request of Miss Mumford, the Commandant of Kent 30, Sandgate, the detachment was ordered to take up duty at the Bevan Hospital, Sandgate, and the equipment and funds were handed over to that hospital.

Between sixty and seventy people from Hythe work at the hospital during the twenty-four hours, besides some gentlemen who act as orderlies.

Commandant—MISS CICELY DALE.
Medical Officers—
DRS. A. R. DAVIS, C. HACKNEY, H. SCOONES.
Lady Superintendents—
MRS. STEWART-HARRIS AND SISTER E. BARTER.
Quartermasters—MRS. HILDYARD, MISS NICHOLETTES.

Members.—Audrey Adam ; Edith Adam ; Julia Ager ; Margaret Andrews ; Dorothy Ashworth ; Marjorie Ashworth ; Mary Avill ; Margaret Barclay ; Beatrice Barlow ; Ethel Barlow, Rosabelle Brandreth ; May Buttanshaw ; Jennie Carter, Edna Chadwick ; Vera Chapman ; Amy Crane ; Muriel Crane ; Kathleen Cutts ; Irene Dale ; Muriel Denniston ; Brenda Dowler ; Florence Drake, Ethel Eastes ; Teresa Floyd ; Mabel Gill ; Ethel Gill-Ballard ; Lilian Hackney ; Muriel Hall ; Edith Hildyard ; Violet Honeywood ; Sarah House ; Alice Lee ; Edith Lewis, Carlota Mackeson ; Elspeth Moubray ; Mildred Murray-Rogers ; Gertrude Noos ; Mary Roach ; Dorothea Ruggles-Brise ; Sybil Schreiber, Ethel Scoones ; Gwenmore Shelford ; Irene Shelley ; Kate Stainer ; Mary Stewart-Harris ; Evelyn Thompson ; Marion Timmins ; Madeline Titley ; Mary Wilks.

KENT 37, GRAVESEND AND NORTHFLEET. The present Commandant was authorised in the early days of the war to raise a men's detachment and within twenty-four hours forty-eight men were on parade and given their first drill. Lectures were given by the medical officer. The detachment was very soon efficient, and with the opening of the Yacht Club Hospital night guard was undertaken and has been carried on continuously. Wounded have been transported into all the hospitals in the district, the Commandant having been put in charge of the transport for the Gravesend district, under the district transport officer, Mrs. E. Bruce-Culver. In addition assistance has been given in other districts. A four-stretcher motor ambulance has been acquired. Many of the members have joined the R.A.M.C.

Commandant—Mr. H. L. Tatham.
Medical Officer—Dr. R. H. Drennan.
Quartermaster—Mr. W. Webster.

Section Leaders.—L. Martin; H. J. Mayo; J. Payne; B. J. Warner.

Members—*D. G. Aitken; E. Ball; F. J. Bennett; A. J. Black; J. W. Boucher; W. Brigham; G. Brooker; T. G. Burberry; H. T. Butler; H. J. Chamberlain; *G. Chatfield; H. Cottam; B. Edmeades; *C. H. Elvin; H. Fairy; W. G. Forder, W. Hames, *J. A. Heath; A. Hook; W. J. Howell, T. Hughes, C. Hurst, S. Johnson; H. Judson; H. V. Kitchen, A. J. Lewis; *A. Mills; George Meakin; J. Parker, W. Parsons, F. Parsons, E. Payne; *F. A. Pittock, C. J. Pusley, *F. A. B. Robinson; A. Roots; *S. Russell, O. Russell, W. D. Sones; *H. M. Thomas; M. Troubridge, *H. K. Tutton, W. A. Webb; *T. Whiston, M. M. Whiting, *H. Winnett, W. Wright; *S. Young.

* Members marked thus have enlisted in His Majesty's Forces

Kent 38. Westerham, was registered in 1911, practices were regularly held, and the detachment was inspected annually by a medical officer from the War Office. Miss Warde was the original

Commandant, but after her marriage the present Commandant was appointed.

On mobilisation a large empty house, "Dunsdale," the property of the family of the late Mr. Norman Watney, was converted into a hospital with fifty beds, and on October 14th everything was ready for the forty-eight Belgian patients who arrived. A motor ambulance, provided by Mr. J. Laird Busk, has been most useful in bringing the more serious cases. The National Service Committee of Westerham has been most generous in giving stores and equipment. Many volunteers have assisted with motors for transport.

Commandant—Miss Watney.
Medical Officer—Dr. J. R. Russell.
Lady Superintendent—Mrs. Marian Perry.
Quartermaster—Miss L. M. Bartlett.

Members —Annie Baker ; Marjorie Beresford ; Isabel Cotton ; Mabel Ford ; Zaidee Holland ; Kate Hooker ; Edith Hughes ; Annie Lewis ; Mabel Maude ; Sylvia Maude ; Mabel McLean ; Edith Pywell ; Edith Rason ; Elizabeth Remnant ; Dorothy Robinson ; Margaret Robinson ; Sarah Robinson ; Sylvia Robinson ; Annie Salmon ; Sylvia Streatfeild ; Catherine Vincent ; Blanche Warde ; Evelyn Warde; Ethel Watney ; Frances White ; Mary Wilkins.

KENT 39, BECKENHAM, has been providing orderlies and transport bearers at the Beckenham hospitals, and doing much useful work. Motorcars have been very generously placed at Beckenham's disposal, and an ambulance wagon has been purchased with local subscriptions.

Commandant—G. G. FIDDES.
Medical Officer—DR. GIDDINGS.
Quartermaster—GEORGE BAXTER.

Section Leaders.—G. A. Piper; F. W. Price, E. W. Sears.

Members.—J. E. Adnams; H. J. Allingham; J. Allingham; A. M. Allison; E. Arnold; J. Bennett; W. S Bolas; J. Britt; J. Brown; W. Burton; J. J Claydon; H. T. Collis, W. H. Dennis; L. B. Finch; H. Friend; E. G. Gilmore; H. Grenyer; L. Hammacott; T. Harris; W. Hatch; W. R Hawkins; A. Ireland; O. M. Kent; G. Knight, P. Knight; E. E. Laws; R. C. Lee; A. Malthouse; A. J. Malthouse, W. E Malthouse, A. Mould; T. H. Oram, F. J. Petri; W. Russell; A. J. Scutcher, H. W. Striko; F. Thornton; S. Thornton; H. A. Tilbrook, W. Treagus, E. Venables; J. Welch; H. Wordsley; T. Young.

KENT 41, BECKENHAM, is a new detachment preparing itself for special work. Ten members belong to the medical profession.

Commandant—DR. STILWELL.
Medical Officer—DR. RANDELL.
Pharmacist—DR. CURTIS.
Quartermaster—DR. TRAPNELL.

Members—D K Allen, H. Austin; Z. Baker; H G Bates; Dr J H Bennett; Dr. H. B Bolus, L Collins, Dr. A. Colyer, J W Cox, L. Crosdale, H. Darby, R Davey; L Deckers; A G. Evans; H. E. Gotelier, A. S. Gotts; W. Gregory, F A. Harrison; W. J. Hatch, A. Hawkes, L D S , C Haywood, G. Herzfeld, Dr J. L Hewlett; M Houghton, C H Hunt, H. B Jones; N. Kent; S. Kingston, Dr. A N. Leathem; G Lee, C Lidgey; F.

Lintot ; J. H. Lowcock ; S. L. Martin ; F. Milligan ; S. Moor ; D. Nottle ; A E. Nunn, M.P S. ; D. J. Penn ; J. H. Redding ; S. B. Stenning ; S Stebbing , — Stoyle ; F. O. Tindley ; Dr F. Todd ; W. B. Trafford ; A. Wallace ; H. Warcup ; C. T. Watts ; E. Wedekind ; L. Whelpton ; A. H. Wood.

KENT 42, GRAVESEND, was the latest effort of the Gravesend detachments ; they had already established two hospitals, one at All Hallows, the other at the Yacht Club.

On October 15th, these being filled with Belgian wounded, the long-disused Rosherville Hotel was taken as a hospital and quickly filled up. Each of the many rooms was allocated to a voluntary worker, who was responsible for its furnishing, and the hospital was completed without any call being made upon any funds, local or county. Since the opening of the hospital there has been a steady flow of patients through the wards.

Under the skilled hands of the consulting surgeon many surgical cases have been successfully dealt with in the small but perfectly appointed operating theatre. A motor ambulance has been added to the equipment. The nursing staff has become most efficient. The Commandant has charge of the transport work for the three big centres of Gravesend, Chatham and Faversham ; the distribution of wounded being undertaken by Doctor Skinner for the first two groups, and Dr.

Prideaux Selby for Faversham. Mr. W. R. Bruce-Culver is the County Secretary for Kent.

Commandant—EDITH BRUCE-CULVER.

Superintendent—ELIZABETH MARGARET WATERMAN.

Quartermaster—IRENE BINGHAM GADD.

Medical Officers—DRS. CHARLES OUTRED,
CHARLES FIRTH, HUBERT SELLS.

Chaplain—REV. SAMUEL POOLE, M.A.

Dentist—WILLIAM EDMONDS, L.D.S. ENG.

Quartermaster (attached)—WILLIAM EDWARD CLIFFORD.

Secretary—WINIFRED DRAYSON.

President of Ladies' Association—
HELENA WESTHORP.

Members.—Fanny Alcock; Jessie Ashdown; Rosalinde Baker; Nellie Beadle; Dorothy Bailey; Ellen Bentley, Dorothea Blake; May Bond; Ethel Brailsford; Louisa Brinkman; Carrie Burleigh; Caroline Carter, Doris Cox, Elsie Douglas; Sophie Dowker; Margery Drayson, Annie Elliot; Hilda Gadd; Louisa Gibson, Winifred Gould; Edith Grandfield; Amy Green; Mary Halford, Ada Hills; Marjorie Hopkins; Kathleen Horrigan; Jessie Jones, Fanny King, Kate Legge; Madeline Legge, Marion Lelean; Alice Lott; Mary Mainwaring; Kathleen Martin; Eileen Mason; Florence Mason, Kathleen Mason; Mary Measures; Monica Morris; Amy Mortlock; Freda Nettlengham, Olive Orpin; Mary Pack; Lucy Penrose; Edith Porter, May Price; Ethel Robinson, Ruth Scriven; Enid Sells, Muriel Shute; Kathleen Simmonds, Mabel Solly; Emily Stones, Ellen Stringer, A Timson; Annie Utting; Elsie Utting, Florence Walker, Edith Ward; Dorothy Waring; Emily Wellard, Evelyn Wheeler, Gertrude Whiting, Francis Wicks; May Wicks, Mabel Williams, Ethel Winder, Susan Winder; Mercy Wise, Dorothy Withers, Ivy Wray

Superintendent of Laundry—Fanny Gould.

Cook Superintendent—Grace Berry

Steward—Ethel Francis.

Orderly Officer.—Doris Rowlstone

KENT 43, FOLKESTONE, was organised at the commencement of the war as the " Civic Guard," instruction in infantry and stretcher drill being given. In September the Guard became a men's voluntary aid detachment.

A course of lectures on first aid was given by Dr. Searle and practices were carried out.

The detachment was mobilised on October 14th, and in conjunction with the fire brigade (of which the Commandant is chief officer) has assisted the R.A.M.C. with the transport of wounded soldiers at Folkestone from hospital ships to all hospitals, V.A.D., civil, and military. In this connection Captain Brandreth Gibbs, Assistant County Director for No. 5 Division, has rendered great assistance.

Commandant—MR. H. O. JONES.
Medical Officer—DR. P. G. SEARLE.
Quartermaster—MR. W. C. MARSH.

Members —F. E G. Bailey; W. B. Banks; J. E. Black; J. Boorman; A. Buttress; A. J. Camburn; R Chambers; S Chittenden, W. W. Cladingbowl; J. A. Clark; H. V. Croucher; J. F. Cunningham; G. F. Davies; J. H. Fox; W. J. Hall; C. Hart; E. J. A. Hart; W. Hilder; A. V. Hoad; A. Howlett; C. O. Humphrey; H. F. Jackson; P Laws; L. W. May; W. H. May; A. L. McLaren; J. Newble; L E Owen; R W. Parfit; L. Payne; J. T. Poole, A. E. Powell; W. E. Saunders; C. Simpson; E H Smith; J. Spencer; S. Stonham; F. E. Tiddy; S. Tunbridge; J. W. Walton; F. Ward; L. Wells; P. J. Whitehead; A J. Whiting; A. Woods; F. Worsley.

KENT 44, TONBRIDGE, was organised in 1911. On the declaration of war, emergency classes were held, and working parties were formed, a room at the Castle being lent by the Urban Council as a depôt. A finance committee, with Mrs. Cazalet, Mrs. Goldsmid and Miss R. Turnbull as officers, collected between £700 and £800 for hospital work.

On October 15th the detachment was mobilised and Quarry Hill House, lent by Mr. J. F. W. Deacon, J.P., was ready for occupation by the evening, and the first party of forty-seven wounded Belgians was quickly installed the same night.

An operating theatre was fitted up by voluntary contributions. The X-ray apparatus of the Tonbridge Cottage Hospital has been placed at the disposal of the detachment.

The honorary medical staff consists of the whole of the Tonbridge medical practitioners. The Red Cross office, under the superintendence of Mrs. Newton and Mrs. Furley, has been opened in the High Street for the reception of gifts for the hospital.

Commandant—Miss J. R. Taylor.
Medical Officer—Dr. Isaac Newton.
Lady Superintendent—Miss Topham.
Quartermaster—Mrs. Jukes.
Assist. Quartermaster—Miss G. Pilditch.
Hon. Dentist—Mr. H. W. Tice.

Members—Daisy Beeching; Hilda Beeching, Nellie Beeching; Marjory Bignold; Mary Blackden, Emene Bullen; Flora Campbell; Grace Clough; Margaret Clough, Violet Collins,

Kato Dain ; Mary Dain ; Blanche Evans ; Evelyn Gaimes ; Lilla Germain ; Alicia Grice ; Mary Harmer ; Isabella Henderson ; Margaret Henson ; May Hicks ; Agnes Howes ; Cecilia Jaquet ; Edith Johnson ; Sybil Johnson ; Annie Jukes ; Sarah Kirby ; Annie Kitchin ; Fadys Le Fleming ; Margaret Lloyd ; Hilda McGeagh ; Ethel McNeil ; Bertha Milner ; Jeannie Murray ; Kathleen Newton ; Mary Palin ; Florence Peake ; Mary Pennell ; Constance Quin ; Minnie Shaul ; Daisy Slight ; May Thyne ; Edith Topham ; Evelyn Turnbull ; Ruth Turnbull ; Grace Venning ; Daisy Walton ; Ivy Walton ; Lilian White.

KENT 45, CHATHAM, is a newly formed men's detachment of 48 members.

Commandant—CAPT. C. D. LEVY.
Medical Officer—DR. G. SKINNER.
Quartermaster—C. LINK.   *Secretary*—A. WILLIAMS.

KENT 45 (*attached*), GILLINGHAM. The members of the Fire Brigade have been keenly interested and successful in ambulance work for many years. Chief Officer Plewis holds the medal of the "Life Saving Society of France," and acts as Secretary to this new and alert detachment.

Commandant—GEORGE PEDDLE.
Medical Officer—DR. E. C. WARREN.
Quartermaster—ERNEST C. READ.
Pharmacist—GEORGE WILLIAM KENNEY.

Section Leaders.—E. Annett ; E. P. Bines ; G. H. Hillisley ; W. J. Young.   *Secretary.*—W. Plewis.

KENT 46, ELHAM, was first initiated by Miss Hordern, meetings for instruction and practice being held. On the departure of Miss Hordern from Elham in the spring of 1914 the present Commandant took charge.

The detachment was mobilised on October 16th and received instructions to prepare a hospital at the Parish Room, offered rent free by the vicar, and at the adjoining house, with a total accommodation for fourteen patients. The furniture and beds were lent by the inhabitants of Elham, and friends at Barham contributed to the equipment, the Elham organisation for the relief of the wounded also supplying a large part. The vicar was responsible for the firing and lighting of the Parish Room. Invaluable help was given by the members of the Elham Men's Fellowship.

On October 26th the first party of twelve wounded Belgians arrived from the trenches.

Commandant—Miss MABEL S. HARRIS.
Medical Officer—DR. HENDERSON.
Lady Superintendent—MRS. DENNIS.
Quartermaster—MISS MERCER.

Members.—Ruth Buon; Emily Chandler, Dorothy File; Elsie Gansby, Elizabeth Gatehouse; Dorothy Gellatly, Frances Hubble, Louisa Jones; Effie Meakin; Monica Mercer; Evelyn Moore Lane, Tina Palmer; Cicely Sheppard; Susan Whitnall, Georgette Williams

KENT 47, BECKENHAM. Formed by Major Bennett in February, 1915, to work in connection with the Women's Detachment, No. 132, at Brooklyn Hospital, Sydenham.

Commandant—MAJOR BENNETT, V.D.
Medical Officer—DR. JAMES GILCHRIST.
Quartermaster—J. H. HAYES.
Pharmacist—A. B. MAKEPEACE.

Members.—I. T. Baguley; S. Baxter; F. Baxter; J. W. Bennett; W. M. Boag; A. Brown, C. T. Dalton; F. C. Deane; C. Edmonds; E. Garratt; A. Harwood; H. Hayes; H. D. Jameson; H. Jordan; F. C. Kessell; J. Parker; C. Short; G. Small; C. Tilliam; J. Tilliam; L. Webster.

KENT 48, ASHFORD. On the outbreak of war a local Committee was called together to prepare for emergencies and to collect funds (£320 was eventually received). The detachment started surgical working parties, and prepared as a hospital the Congregational schoolroom (lent by Rev. G. H. Russell and his deacons) with accommodation for forty beds. The small ward in this building was opened on October 14th for sick Territorials, and on October 22nd the first party of Belgians arrived; since then three more convoys of Belgians have passed through the wards.

The work of the hospital has been chiefly amongst the local troops, for whom no other hospital is available. Over three hundred patients in all have been treated. There are seventy members, including three trained nurses.

Mr. Fitz Hugh has charge of the important transport work for the Ashford group of hospitals, and sincere thanks are expressed to him for much self-denying labour; also to Mr. Gregg, of Kent 11, who has acted as honorary steward; and the members of Kent 11 and 13 for help with night orderly work. Also to Miss Pledge, of "Contingent" K 48, for much-valued help.

Commandant—MRS. I. M. BUCKLAND.
Medical Officer—DR. COLVILLE.
Lady Superintendent—MRS. COKE.
Quartermaster—MISS KNOCK.
Assist. Quartermaster—MISS THORPE.

Members—Madge Adams; Margaret Avery; Dora Bailey; Kathleen Bailey; Vera Baker; Violet Barker; Naomi Bates; Dorothy Bennett; Olivia Broadbank, Annie Burrows; Violet Catchpole; Augusta Chantler; Christina Chapman; Ethel Chapman; Violet Cheeksfield, Frances Mary Clapson, Hilda Cooper; Gladys Cox, Ada Crux; Nance Daniel; Nellie Davis; Marie De Luze; Carey Down; Irene Down; Katherine Down; Victoria Down; Frances Edwards-Ker (Trained Nurse), Constance Elliot; Julia Fenn; Madeline Halloran; Bridget Jemmett, Mary Jennings; Elsie Kingsford; Evelyn Kingsford, Hilda Kingsnorth; Katherine Leigh Pemberton; May Leigh Pemberton; Mary Lewis, Ethel Luckhurst, Dorothy Mallion; Jessie Morton; Norah Morton; Dorothy Neal; Marjorie Oakley; Margaret Oliver; May Pickering, Ellen Pullen; Lily Quested; Elizabeth Quick; Laura Slingleton; Rachel Shorter; Kate Skelton (Trained Nurse); — Standen, Kate Tapley, Edith Wellard.

K

Recruits.—Dorothy Beaney ; Katharine Beck ; Dorothy Butler ; Gertrude May Caffeyn ; Kathleen Margaret Creery ; Nellie Godden ; — Norie ; Edith Porter ; Ida Scott ; Mildred Scott ; Alberta Treadwell ; Elizabeth Laura Treadwell ; Ethel Waters ; Madge Wickham ; Bertha Williams ; Irene Wind ; Muriel Gertrude Winthrop.

KENT 50, BROMLEY COMMON, KESTON AND HAYES, was started in 1912.

In the previous year Lady Lubbock arranged classes in Red Cross work at her house, and it was at these classes that the older members qualified. At the outbreak of war the detachment worked for a time at the Bromley Cottage Hospital.

Mobilisation took place on October 13th, 1914, and most of the beds were occupied by Belgian soldiers on the following day.

There are three hospitals under the care of this detachment :

1. Bloomfield Road, Bromley Common, kindly lent by the trustees of the Primitive Methodist Schools, with twenty-five beds.

2. "The Rookery," Bromley Common, where Mr. and Mrs. A. C. Norman are kindly lending three large rooms with eighteen beds.

3. "Lodore," Mason's Hill, where Mr. and Mrs. Hennah take in seven patients, free of all expense.

The detachment has received much willing help and many useful gifts, including a number of valuable instruments for surgical work.

Thanks to the further generosity of Mr. A. C. Norman a new large hospital with an operating theatre and fifty beds has been opened at "Oakley" in place of the present main building.

There is at this hospital an installation for hot-air treatment for joint diseases ; also a complete equipment for electrical massage.

The honorary consulting surgeons are Frank Kidd, Esq., F.R.C.S., Richard Warren, Esq., F.R.C.S., Lewis Smith, Esq., M.D., and Dr. Daley, anæsthetist, the surgeons and physicians respectively of the London Hospital.

The kitchen arrangements are directed by Mrs. Harris, head cook, Mrs. Craster and Miss Cooling. Very valuable assistance with the accounts has been rendered by Mr. Gilliard.

Two hundred and forty patients have passed through the hospitals.

Commandant—MISS MADGE BOOSEY.
Medical Officer—DR. CRASTER.
Lady Superintendent—MISS A. SANDLE.
Quartermaster—MISS M. CLOWES.
Assist. Quartermaster—MISS R. LUBBOCK.

Members—Gertrude Allen, May Anderson; Gertrude Atkinson, Enid Boosey, Sarah Clifford, Kate Cooling; Mary Craster, Marian Dann, Cicely Dodgson, Laura Fox; Rosa Garrard, Kate Garrard, Catherine Harris; Louisa Hawkings, Nellie Heathcote, Amy Hutchinson; Edith Lawrence, Hilda Lubbock; Dorothy Lubbock, Mildred Lubbock, Madeline Lenox Conyngham, Edith Memess;

Hilda Murphy; Mary Norman; Virginia Norman; Doris Potter; Beryl Ritter; Gertrude Sandle; Elizabeth Slessor; Sarah Smith; Barbara Stiles; Elsie Trevor; Mary Tucker; Irene Wheeler-Bennett; Grace Wood; Lelia Wright.

KENT 52, BROMLEY. The members of this detachment—the earliest formed in Bromley—have been actively engaged since 1910, and upon the outbreak of war in August, 1914, well-thought-out preparations were made by the Commandant for equipping a hospital.

When, therefore, the dual order to mobilise and prepare a hospital was received, the Masonic Hall, previously promised by the Directors, became the centre of the detachment's activities.

Within half an hour about two dozen members paraded, some of whom were dispatched to collect equipment which various friends had promised, and for this purpose Mr. George Pyrke of High Street, Bromley, kindly lent a motor-van.

By 2 a.m. on Wednesday, October 14th, the members were to be seen scrubbing the floors and putting up the beds. Before 12 noon twenty-seven beds were ready, and three hours later these were occupied by wounded Belgian soldiers.

Thus the hall, which would otherwise have been the scene of an important Masonic gathering that evening, was transformed into a hospital, showing the sad and cruel results of modern warfare.

Steps were taken for equipping two extra

wards; storerooms, an operating theatre, have been arranged, and the accommodation is now complete for forty-seven patients. In addition to the main hospital several important annexes have been available through the generosity of neighbouring residents, as follows :

Mr. T. C. Dewey, in addition to entirely providing in the Cottage Hospital the ward which bears his name, has arranged the pavilion in his garden as two splendid wards, capable of taking twelve patients. Miss Davies and Miss Larkin are in charge.

Mr. A. H. K. Squire gave up the greater part of his residence, " Whitegarth," for the reception of fourteen patients, and Mrs. Squire, with the assistance of other ladies, generously provided for the wounded under care at this hospital.

Mr. Coles Child gave up part of Bromley Palace, his residence, and Mrs. Coles Child and her daughters undertook the nursing of eight patients during the rush in the earlier days.

Mr. and Mrs. A. M. Rogers have entirely provided twelve beds at their house, " Langley Wood," and have been most kind and successful in their efforts.

Mr. and Mrs. P. Boyd have also unselfishly given up a part of their house at 21 Holwood Road and have continuously cared for twelve patients.

Mr. and Mrs. H. D. Kelf have kindly supplied four beds at No. 88 Hayes Road.

The detachment is greatly indebted to the Lady Superintendent, Miss Ada Boss, for the valuable services which she has freely and unsparingly given at all times of the day and night; also to Mrs. Whittle and her band of workers for self-denying duty in the kitchens. Best thanks are expressed to Mr. Temple West and to Mrs. Peill for much kindly consideration of the patients' needs.

Commandant—MISS ETHEL A. COAD.
Medical Officer—DR. R. MONTGOMERY.
Lady Superintendent—MISS ADA BOSS.
Quartermaster—MRS. J. H. YOLLAND.

Members.—Margaret Anderson; Norah Atkinson; Marjory Best; Dorothy Bradshaw; Joan Cardwell; Zoe Carey; Doris Carr; Audrey Coles Child; Florence Covell; Edith Darby; Irene Doxford; Helen Durbridge, Kathleen Ellis; Marjory Ellis; Gwendolen Evans; Evelyn Fischer; Lily Gunton; Lucy Hall; Minnie Hawkings; Nellie Heaysman; Helen Hemus; Lucy Jenyns; Louisa Larkins, Mary Lewis; Florence Milloy; Norah Myers, Agatha Nicholson; Margaret Nicholson; Ethel Payne; Emily Peill; Elsie Pope; Dora Prechtel; Winifred Quelch; Louise Rayden; Hilda Rogers; Irene Rogers; Louise Rossell, Stella Sanderson; Eleanor Satherthwaite; Bessie Silver; Doris Slipper; Kathleen Thompson; Dorothy Tilling; Annie Walters; Edith Walthew. Grace Weller; Amy Whittle; Gertrude Whittle; Hilda Wilkins; Roma Wood.

Elstree Hospital, Bromley, is worked in connection with Kent 52.

After " Whitegarth " was given up, Mr. Medcalf generously offered " Elstree," a beautifully situated house near by. Here a first-class hospital, complete in every detail, has been formed. There are twenty-three beds and a fully-equipped operating theatre.

The hospital is managed by a committee: Messrs. C. Shaw Lovell, Chairman ; E. W. Tilling ; W. Howard Wood ; T. Durbridge, Junr. ; A. H. K. Squire ; W. Sommerville ; Egerton C. Lovell ; Ernest Durbridge, Treasurer ; Bertram Hellyer, Secretary.

The staff consists of Colonel D'Arcy Power, Honorary Consulting Surgeon ; Dr. Alfred E. Price, Honorary Medical Officer ; Miss Holmes, the sister in charge ; Miss Sparkes, the night nurse ; assisted by Mrs. Ernest Durbridge, Mrs. Bertram Hellyer, Mrs. Egerton Lovell, Mrs. Edward Medcalf, Mrs. Sommerville, Mrs. Squire, Mrs. Tilling, and Mrs. Howard Wood, forming the Ladies' Committee; also Miss Dorothy Bartrum, Miss Eleanor Bruce, Mrs. George Codd, Miss Marguerite Cunéo, Miss Florence Durbridge, Mrs. Hubert Faber, Mrs. Vernon Lovell, Mrs. Ernest Potter, Miss Isabel Potter, Miss Marian Tatham, and Mrs. Thorpe.

KENT 54, BROMLEY, came into being in March, 1912, and at once frequent meetings were started for instruction in Red Cross work, many members being able to gain practical experience in nursing in the wards of the Marylebone Infirmary and the Bromley Cottage Hospital. Field days were held, and the camps at Herne and Rolvenden were well attended.

On October 14th, at 2 a.m., a message was received to prepare accommodation for wounded, and St. Mary's Church Hall, kindly lent by Rev. W. Gowans and his Church Hall Committee, was quickly prepared as a V.A.D. hospital.

Alderman G. Weeks installed a bath, and geysers were lent by the S. Suburban Gas Co. Vans, kindly lent by Messrs. Soans and Son and Humerston and Co., collected equipment promised by friends, and by 12 noon the wards were cleaned, furnished, and were ready to receive the first convoy of wounded. In two days the number of patients had risen to sixty-five.

Apart from the care and skill bestowed on the patients by the late Medical Officer, Dr. Cyril Ilott (who has now taken up Army medical duties), the sisters and members, the food is all cooked by voluntary members on the premises.

An excellent operating theatre has been installed, owing to the generosity of friends, with an operating table and high-pressure steriliser.

A long verandah has been given and erected, and motor owners have freely given the use of their cars. They have also conveyed the patients to London for the special treatment kindly accorded by Dr. Gustave Hamel.

In the earlier stages of the war Mrs. Loly most generously furnished Quernmore School Infirmary as an extra hospital, and still holds the same fully prepared in case of future emergencies. It is only just to record that much valuable assistance has been given to this detachment by Colonel Lewin.

Commandant—Mrs. Lewin.
Medical Officers—Dr. A. C. Haslam,
Dr. Herbert Ilott, Dr. Henshaw.
Lady Superintendent—Mrs. Noakes.
Quartermaster—Miss D. Tweedy.

Members —Dorothy Addiscott; Ella Addiscott; Winifred Addiscott; Annie Airey; Alice Alston; Enid Atkinson; Gladys Bourner; Rene Bourner; Ruth Buck; May Grant Burls, Harriet M. Carlyon, Nellie Cave; Zoe Cave; Estelle Clarke; Ella Cossins, Ethel Cowen; Gertrude Dale; Millie Darby; Henrietta Denney; Mary Draper; Adeline Edwards, Dorothy Elliott; Ethel Ellman; E. A Findlay; Elise Flint; Marjorie Forman; Dorothy France, Joyce Gayford; Violet Gibbs; Christiania Greenhill; G. M. L. Griffith; Joan Hay, Dorothy Henwood, Ethel Henwood; Marjorie Henwood; Edith Holtom, Dorothea Lewin, Mary March; Kate Marlow; Vera Mead; Grace Moger, Maude Moore, Hilda Munday; Emily Part, Eva Peachey; Mabel Peachey, Helen Porteous, Norah Ransom; Violet Richardson, Ruth Richardson; Mabel Ridley, Maud Sharp; Mary Sketchley; Kathleen Stahlschmidt, Marjorie Stokes; Ivy Sutton; Edith Trimmer, Gertrude Vasey; Marjorie Weyman; Nellie Wilson

KENT 54 (*attached*), SHORTLANDS. The Parish

Room, Shortlands, was opened on October 22nd, 1914, as a hospital. The staff is drawn from ladies of the neighbourhood who had previously passed their examinations, and is under the charge of Nurse Hooper. Local ladies worked hard to prepare the hospital, and the residents have freely sent gifts both in money and kind.

Commandant and Medical Officer—
DR. HAWKE.
*Lady Superintendent—*MISS F. BONNER.
Quartermasters—
MRS. HAWKE AND MRS. STAHLSCHMIDT.

Members.—Mabel Cohen ; Madge Eglington ; Lavinia Evelyn-Jones ; Iris Gill ; Margaret Grantham ; Mary Harley-Thomas ; Evelyn Hewetson ; Mabel Klaber ; Eileen Lanham ; Kathleen Lloyd ; Susan Mackie ; Constance Payne ; Edith Scobell ; Annie Stubbs ; Evelyn Taylor ; Florence Temple ; Lilian Walker.

KENT 56, SEVENOAKS, was first formed by the Honourable Victoria Sackville West. Early in 1913 the detachment had outgrown its capacity and was divided, Kent 76 then being formed under Mrs. Hilder.

Later in the same year Miss Sackville West resigned and the present Commandant took charge.

In August, 1914, the detachment increased its activities, and on October 14th mobilisation orders were received. St. John's Sunday School room was quickly prepared as a hospital, and the first convoy of Belgian wounded was installed.

The hospital has room for fifty cases, and an operating theatre has been fitted up.

Many valuable gifts have been received from Lady Sackville, Mr. Robert Mond, and many others.

Commandant—MISS AUREA LAMBARDE.
Medical Officer—DR. STERRY.
Lady Superintendent—NURSE DUNN.
Quartermaster—MRS. SMITHERS.

Members.—Elinor Baddeley; Queenie Battiscombe; Ruby Battiscombe; Violet Battiscombe; Agnes Beake, Mary Boyd; Marjorie Campbell; Lisa Carnell, Marjorie Crawford, Guhelma Deane, Fanny Dodd; Elfrida Dunkerley; Jessie Ellman; Beatrice Evans, Evelyn Fawcett, Emmeline Gibson, Adeline Harmer; Mabel Kraftmeier; Helen Laurie; Emily Loveland; Marjorie Pittar; Olive Rubens, Lilian Sills, Margaret Sills; Mollie Smithers; Constance Stamp, Lilian Swanzy, Delia Tierney; Ethel Whebby, Joyce Wright.

KENT 58, CHEVENING, was formed four years ago. The hospital was opened on October 14th, when thirty Belgians were admitted. There were then two buildings in use, Chipstead Mission Hall and Chipstead Place, lent by Mr. Duveen for three months. Besides men from overseas, local troops have been admitted.

Generous gifts have been received, support coming even from Australia and America. The regular staff has been greatly increased. Much valuable assistance has been received from ambulance men. As Chipstead Place is now closed there is only one ward of thirty-two beds, but a kind anonymous friend of the hospital is having an annexe built to the Mission Hall which will greatly augment the accommodation.

Commandant—Miss BERYL HALL-HALL.

Vice-Commandant—ETHEL VOELCKER.

Medical Officer—DR. J. F. ALEXANDER.

Assistant Medical Officer—DR. MACARTNEY.

Lady Superintendent—NURSE BEVAN.

Quartermaster—A. SHILBECK.

Assistant Quartermaster—CARA HALL-HALL.

Sisters—BEAVAN, M. DAVIES, STEVENS.

Nurses and Nursing Orderlies —Elizabeth Ansell; B. Auckorn; Norah Arnott; Sarah Breething; Elizabeth Booker; Mary Burfoot; Florence Campell; Annie Clarke; Alice Conell; Florence Carter, E Dark; Florence Drake; Phyllis Detelebach; Ethel Gold; Isabella Gold; Ethel Glazier, Annie Hamlin; Claretta King; Muriel King; Faith Laurence; Phyllis Meyerstein; Enid Mort; Dorothy Punter; Helen Riall; Nellie Smith; Winifred Smythe; Toy Snartt; Beatrice Turnell; Cicely Wreford; Frances Wreford; Kathleen Wreford; Diana Wreford; Gertrude White.

Kitchen Staff.— — Bashford; A. Cole; Mildred Costen; —Dark, Helen Dumere; Joan Dumere; — Flint; De C. Godfrey, — Hubble; Joan Hounsome; Emily Jackson; — Jobson; Norah King; Jane Lewis; Margaret Mort; D. Peters, — Pinher; Elizabeth Polhill-Drabble; — Rocheling, — Rogers; Dorothy Rayner, Alice Scott; Caroline Stocking; — Smith; — Waller; J. Waller

Assistant Night Nurses.— — Bichley and — Carrie-Smith.

Permanent Orderly.—J. Robson.

R A.M.C. Orderlies.— — Farrell; — Shard; — Savage.

Scouts from Dunton Green and Brasted.

KENT 60, CHISLEHURST. In May, 1912, a meeting was called by Dr. Allan, to consider the advisability of forming a voluntary aid detachment in the neighbourhood, and Kent 60 was the outcome, with Miss Alston as Commandant. Miss Alston resigned in the following September, and the present Commandant took charge.

In the Yolland shield competition of 1913 the detachment gained over 90 per cent marks, and was awarded a prize stretcher ; while during the 1914 camp the composite detachment, of which Kent 60 formed a part, won the silver challenge bowl.

Throughout August and September, 1914, the detachment worked hard to prepare the necessary equipment for a hospital, and members were able to gain some practical experience at the local civil hospital.

Orders to mobilise were received at midnight on October 13th, and Christ Church Hall with twenty-five beds was ready for occupation by 6 a.m. the next day. The first convoy of thirty-three Belgians was received at 9 a.m., the slighter cases being sent to " Coed Bel," where Miss Fox kindly lent the sanatorium with eight beds. Mrs. Gibson acted as trained nurse by day and Miss Gibson by night. After two days instructions were received to prepare for more patients, and Abbey Lodge was equipped as a hospital ; the second convoy of thirty Belgians arriving on October 17th.

The initial difficulties of preparing this hospital

were great, as the house had been long empty, but it is specially adapted for its present use as it is built on institutional lines.

Dr. Brennan performed much excellent work at the outset of affairs.

The services of Sister Treasure and Nurse North have been much appreciated.

Christ Church Hospital was moved to " Brooklyn," lent by Mr. Acton Garle, during the winter.

The late Mr. William Willett was instrumental in obtaining the use of Abbey Lodge for a year rent free from Mr. Erskine of Ryde. The Rev. G. H. Pole gave his Parish Room at great inconvenience, and Mr. George Croll has been most generous and has taken unfailing interest in the hospital, while Mr. Straus has kindly helped with the accounts. The residents of Chislehurst have helped considerably with contributions. Two hundred and forty-nine patients have been cared for in the hospitals.

Commandant—Miss Beatrix Batten.
Medical Officer—Dr. Allan.
Deputy Medical Officer—Dr. Lawson.
Quartermaster—Miss L. Pole.

Members.—Theodora Adamson ; Winifred Alston ; Dorothy Batten ; Margaret Cadell ; Evaline Clark ; Elsie Doran ; Elizabeth Fanner ; Ellen Dorothy Forest, Doris Greeff ; Grace Greengrass ; Janet Joyce ; Lilian Knight, Lucy A Maccall ; Annie O'Brien ; Honor O'Brien ; Luisa Page ; Marjorie Pattisson ; Gladys Pole ; Hilda Pole ; Muriel Pole, Ellen Pott ; Elaine Powell, Kathleen Powell, May Rena Wilson.

Supernumeraries.—Dagmar Bennett; Eileen Bennett; Mrs.
Good, Suzanne Good; Dora Howard; Edith Margetson;
Agnes McFarlane; Edith Murton; Agnes Paterson;
Dorothy Payne; Marian de Quincey; Doris Scarch;
Dorothy Warrington; Norah Webb; Jessie Whyte; Marjorie Whyte.

KENT 62, SIDCUP, was started in 1912 on the initiative of Dr. George Davis.

On the declaration of war the officers of the Congregational Church, Sidcup, freely offered their lecture hall and school premises to be arranged as a hospital to contain thirty-four beds in three wards. The whole of the furniture was lent locally, and a generous gift of equipment was received from the Working Guild of the Congregational Church. Six trained nurses have given their services voluntarily.

A fourth ward has now been added, by the kindness of the Wesleyan Church in lending their school premises, to hold sixteen beds, bringing the total up to fifty.

Dr. Davis having gone to the front, the present Medical Officer has been appointed.

Commandant—MRS. REED.
Medical Officer—DR. T. D. MILLER.
Lady Superintendent—MISS FINCH.
Quartermaster—MRS. DAWBARN.

Members.—Gladys Anderson, Violet Anderson; Annie Atkinson; Alexandra Balls; Ada Beale; Florence Beale; Lizzie

Braund ; Rose Callender ; Edith Chiltern ; Minnie Close ; Marion Cross ; George Dalton ; Rosa Dalton ; Edith Davidson ; Eleanor Davis ; Amys Easten ; Leila Eley ; Evelyn Elliott ; Florence Farnfield ; Marjory Fletcher ; Isabel Foster ; Theresa Foster ; Jessie Harries ; Audrey Hewitt ; Mary Horten ; Maud Jenkins ; Emily Membrey ; Amy Millard ; Mary Palmer ; Florence Parsons ; Dulcie Rackham ; Joyce Rayment ; Madge Ross , Mildred Rowbotham ; Carrie Snelling ; Dorothy Stevenson ; Amy Townend ; Mary Wells ; Elsie Wilkinson ; Winifred Wilkinson ; Gwenthllian Williams ; Agnes Woodcock ; Elsie Young.

KENT 64, WESTGATE, was formed in 1912. Mobilised on October 14th, 1914, fifty-two Belgian soldiers were received in the early morning of the following day at Quex Park, Birchington, the private residence of Major and Mrs. Powell-Cotton.

On November 4th the detachment moved to " High Beach," Westgate, taking with them the wounded then under treatment. This house, then standing empty, was lent by the trustees of the late Mrs. du Pré Thornton as a temporary hospital, with accommodation for forty-seven patients. The whole of the equipment was provided by the people of the neighbourhood.

A local fund subscribed in the neighbourhood was placed at the disposal of the detachment with a representative Committee to control it.

On January 5th the Medical Officer, Dr. Rutherford, joined the R.A.M.C., and the present Medical Officer was appointed.

Commandant—MRS. STAVELEY.
Medical Officer—DR. HEATON.
Lady Superintendent—MISS KENNEDY.
Quartermaster—MISS COWL-PAYNE.

Members.—Fanny Burchell ; Agnes Cazalet ; Constance Cowl-Payne , Ethel Cross , Vyvyan Davies , Ada Grant ; Dorothy Hubbard ; Florence Ingram ; Hilda Ingram ; Mary Isted ; Ada Kennedy ; Muriel Klaber ; Eveline Knowles ; Mary Muncey ; Aline North , Ella Rogers ; May Rogers ; Ada Rowe ; Ethel Stringer , Ethel Sugden ; Bessie Teetgen ; Agnes Towers , Ethel Wright.

KENT 66, CHISLEHURST. In July, 1913, the Chislehurst detachment had become so large that it was thought desirable that two detachments should be made, and No. 66 was then formed.

Much work had been done in obtaining promises of the loan of houses and equipment, and the lists were fortunately so complete that on mobilisation everything was ready. Late on October 13th the detachment was called up ; Holbrook House was taken over, scrubbed and fitted up complete as a hospital with thirty-five beds by 5 a.m. At 9 a.m. thirty-five Belgians were received. On October 16th orders were given to prepare another hospital, and Hornbrook House was equipped with accommodation for fifty patients, and by the 26th the two hospitals contained ninety-three patients. Since then the hospitals have undergone many improve-

L

ments, thanks to a host of friends, including the fitting up of a splendid modern operating theatre with a large steriliser.

Friends have freely offered their motors for transport from the station to the hospital. A constant flow of wounded and sick, including men from the Expeditionary Force, has passed through the wards. The Medical Officer has charge jointly with Dr. Sterry of the No. 1 Division of Kent, and much is due to his energy and ability.

Commandant—Mrs. Allan.
Medical Officer—Dr. Allan.
Lady Superintendent—Miss E. Hunter.
Quartermaster—Miss M. Villiers.

Members. — Gladys Allen , Lorna Battiscombe ; Margaret Battiscombe ; Elsie Bosworth ; Sylvia Bosworth ; Nurse Bush , Elsie Christopher ; Annie Clarke ; Louisa Dennis ; Kate Dixon ; Maude Dixon , Mabel Dixon ; Jane Eade ; Nurse Foster, Emily Garrett ; Gwen George , Mary Groombridge ; Aleen Heber-Percy ; Janet James ; Viscountess Edith Kerckhove ; Edith Kerckhove ; Rosita Kerckhove ; Iris King ; Vera King ; Nurse Meech ; Margaret Mens ; Louisa Mudd ; Elsie Nash ; Isabel Nevill ; Dorothy Nicolls ; Florence Nightingale ; Helen Oldendorff ; Agnes Ousley ; Grace Pierce ; Margaret Pinyon ; Mary Pudsey ; Bridget Robinson ; Jessie Sicklemore ; Lucia Slade ; Winifred Thompson ; Sophie Tiarks ; Florence Turner ; Bessie Turner , Evelyn Tylor , Mary Watson ; Winifred Whitehead.
Bath Orderly —Louis Bayman.

KENT 68, SITTINGBOURNE, was formed in 1911 by Colonel Honeyball in conjunction with a committee, of which the Earl of Westmorland was president. On mobilisation the detachment opened the Red Cross hospital in a house lent by Mr. G. H. Dean of Sittingbourne, and has done excellent work since.

Commandant—MRS. HONEYBALL.
Medical Officers—
DRS. BURFORD TAYLOR, C. IND, G. TAUNTON.
Lady Superintendent—MISS SEAL.
Quartermaster—MISS OST.

Members —Bertha Andrews ; Maud Baker; Maud Beriff ; Rose Boucher ; Annie Boulding ; Constance Bullen ; Edith Chesson ; Dorothy Chrisfield ; Victoria Christmas ; Maud Clinch ; Winifred Creagh ; Mary Cremer ; Lily Curry ; Lilian Doubleday ; Lily Fry ; Bertha Gardiner ; Dorothy Gardner , Kate Gates ; Maud Giles ; Frances Goodhew ; Maud Goodhew ; Gladys Grant ; Nora Green ; Dorothy Gunnell ; Jane Holdstock ; Alice Leigh-Pemberton ; Carrie Luckhurst , Laura Meers , Mary Millen , Bertha Nicholls , Ellen Ost , Ellen Palmer ; Florence Palmer ; Ethel Philpotts ; Ellen Reeves , Hilda Reynolds , Esther Ricconimi ; Charlotte Robinson , Agnes Roper ; Dorothy Scoones ; Julia Scoones , Edith Stanley , Olivet Stanton ; Netty Stuart ; Mary Tagert , Henrietta Tarrant , Josephine Tarrant ; Vera Tarrant ; Mary Taunton ; Edith Waddeys ; Agnes Watts

KENT 70, CANTERBURY, was started in 1912 by Miss M. C. Waterfield, through the St. John Ambulance Association. In May, 1914, the detachment became so large that it was divided, Miss Wemyss being made Commandant of the second half, known as Kent 100 V.A.D.

From the beginning of August, 1914, members worked in the Kent and Canterbury Hospital, both in the wards and in the operating theatre. The two detachments, on the outbreak of war, started to prepare a hospital. St. Augustine's College was lent them, and a Red Cross committee was formed to supply funds. On August 11th patients from the local troops were received, but at the commencement of term the College had to be vacated.

Fortunately the detachments were lent two houses, Dane John House by the executors of Miss Wightwick and "Abbotts Barton" by Mr. Bennett Goldney, M.P. for Canterbury. Kent 70 took charge of the first, and Kent 100 took over "Abbotts Barton."

Mobilised on September 19th, the two hospitals were quickly got ready, and patients from the Front were admitted.

Dane John House, in addition to receiving wounded from the Front, has acted as a receiving hospital for the 1st and 3rd West Lancashire Field Ambulance.

Four hundred and forty-eight patients have passed through the two hospitals.

Many kind presents and loans for the equipment and upkeep of the two hospitals have been received.

The first sister-in-charge, Miss Williams, went through the South African War and was afterwards at Woolwich. She was appointed to the Hospital Ship " St. Patrick " in April, 1915.

Commandant—Miss M. C. Waterfield.
Medical Officer—Dr. E. D. Whitehead Reid.
Lady Superintendent—Miss G. Dodgson.
Quartermaster—Miss A. A. Russell.

Members.—Caroline Helena Allardyce; Dorothy Helen Bellars; Florence Bignell; Margaret Blundell; Dorothy Louisa Joan Bremner; Florence Carter; Maud Cattell; Maude Clements; Ethel Kate Cook; Hilda Court; Florence Davies; Kate Denne; Mabel Denne; Bertha Elliott; Cristina Goulden; Elizabeth Gunn; Dorothy Honeyball, Dorothy Ann Hunt; Winifred Hunt; Alice Fredrica Kennedy; Frances Stephanie Kennett; Dorothy Ivy Kimpton; Amy Leathers; Eliza Marshall; Alice Maud Mason; Gertrude Maxted; Margaret Maxted; Leslie Mitchell, Edith Nash; Phyllis Nelson; Beatrice Muriel Norton, Dora Pettit; Stella Pettit; Mabel Pittock; Annie Reay; Cecil Russell; Joan Russell, Mabel Slater; Edith Spicer; Louisa Spinner, Hyacinth Staple; G. Sutton; Bertha Terry; Elena de Vial; Noel Westbury; Helen Mary Williams; Stella Marion Wills.

Kent 72, Sittingbourne, was started in 1912, and the members earnestly prepared themselves for future emergencies.

At the outbreak of war subscriptions were collected, and Trinity Hall. Sittingbourne, was kindly offered by the Rev. C. Eyre Kidson. The detachment was mobilised on October 14th, 1914, and quickly prepared the hall as a hospital. Loans and gifts of equipment in abundance were offered.

One hundred and eighty patients have been treated in the hospital. The Medical Officer is Assistant County Director for No. 4 Division of Kent, and has charge also of the distribution of patients when convoys arrive at Sittingbourne Station.

Commandant—MRS. PRIDEAUX SELBY.
Medical Officer—DR. PRIDEAUX SELBY.
Lady Superintendent—MRS. HENDERSON.
Quartermaster—MISS II. WEBSTER.

Members.—Jessie Apperley ; Beatrice Ayres ; Annie Barling ; Frances Bowles ; Maud Brightman ; Edith Colt-Williams ; Maud Colthup ; Ada Dalton ; Flora Dean ; Maud Dixon ; Elsie Entiknap ; Barbara Filmer ; Edith Filmer ; Winifred Gascoyne ; Annie George ; Amy Gibbings ; Rosa Goodwin ; Ellen Hales ; Madge Hallett ; Clara Harvey , Fanny Houghton ; Hilda Jarvis , Lucy Jarvis ; Isabel Jones ; Beatrice Julian ; Winifred Lefevre , Elsie Mackenzie ; Jean Menter ; Lily Nix , Millie de Pass ; Norah Pillow ; Winifred Piper ; Anna Potts , Mary Prentis ; Alice Purton , Gladys Seager ; Joan Selby ; Isabel Sergent ; Cecilia Sewell ; Elizabeth Street ; Dorothy Strouts ; Helen Thomson ; Eleanor Toulmin ; Annie Vallance ; Bertha Vallance ; Nora Watson ; Mary Wright.

KENT 74, SPELDHURST. Bidborough Court, then standing empty, was placed at the disposal of Kent 74 by Mr. H. J. Wood, and on mobilisation was quickly transformed into a model temporary hospital.

The first call, on Sunday, October 25th, 1914, would have tested the efficiency of a much more

experienced staff, for thirty Belgians were sent at
the shortest notice direct from the trenches at
Dixmude ; but everything was ready, and all was
carried through without a hitch, the Speldhurst
Men's Bearer Squad rendering most useful assistance.

Commandant—Miss K. Pott.
Medical Officer—Dr. Hesketh Biggs.
Lady Superintendent—Miss A. Pumphrey.
Quartermaster—Mrs. Taylor Marsh.

Members.—Jane Allan ; Muriel Apperly ; Kathleen Bartram ;
Julia Belcher ; Dorothy Colley, Adeline Collins ; Nora
Cowley ; Norah Dundas ; Hilda Field, Idaberga Fooks ;
Ursula Hills, Brenda Hopkins ; Griselda Kirk, May Kirk ;
Lisette Lee ; Girlie Lucas ; Henrietta Martin, Nancy
Mason ; Theo Nicholson, Mary Phillpotts ; Evelyn Pott ;
Edith Pulley ; Bertha Silverthorne, Hannah Stone ; Nora
Sweetnam, Ethel Talbot ; Margery Taylor ; Phyllis
Tindall, Doris Walter ; Elsie Warner ; Joy Williams ;
Annslee Winton.

Kent 76, Sevenoaks. From January of 1912
this detachment has been in full swing.

Sevenoaks being a centre for troops, it was
decided on September 18th, 1914, to open for the
use of the R. West Kent Territorials a ward in the
Cornwall Hall. On October 11th this small effort
was greatly enlarged, the whole hospital being
opened, on notification of the arrival of forty-three
wounded Belgians ; and on November 24th the
first convoy of men from the Expeditionary Force
was received. Some of these soldiers were ap-

parently incurable cases, but all have been returned fit for service.

At the beginning of the new year, with the consent of the V.A.D. authorities, the hospital was taken over as a military base hospital for the 2nd West Lancashire Field Ambulance. Since the beginning the work has been carried on most successfully, 221 cases having been dealt with, including a second convoy from the firing line.

The hospital is staffed by thirty V.A.D. members, four trained nurses and a certificated masseuse.

The Honorary Commandant is in charge of the onerous duty of transport for the Sevenoaks section, with Dr. Sterry as distributing officer, and much excellent work has been done.

Commandant and Lady Superintendent—
Mrs. P. Mansfield.

Honorary Commandant—de Barri Crawshay, Esq.
Medical Officer—Dr. P. Mansfield.
Quartermaster—Miss Rosemary Rooker.

Members.—Ethel Amsden . Mabel Anson ; Jessie Ashdown ; Mildred Athill , Mildred Bosanquet , Hester Bull , Jessie Clark ; Elsie Clouting ; Dorothy Coleman ; Emma Crump ; Constance Dennes ; Florence De Ville ; Irene Durrant ; Doris Escombe ; Ethel Hards ; Madge Harrison ; Mary Hay ; Margery Hearson ; Evelyn Heslop ; Gertrude Heslop ; Freda Hilder , Dorothy Limbrick ; Nora Linnell ; Kathleen Madden ; Arthur Martin ; Margaret Martin ; Alex Norman ; Lylie Pearce Clark ; Muriel Pinchin , Elsie Pinnell ; Phyllis Pinnell ; Grace Poland , Judith Poland ; Molly Poole ; Cecil Rooker ; Frances Soyer , Alice Schwartz , Marjorie Sikes ; Mary Standen , Vera Thompson , Irene Westcombe ; Gertrude Winch.

KENT 78, BICKLEY, on mobilisation quickly got to work at " Southwood," Bickley, kindly lent by Mr. Wythes, and on the following two days forty wounded Belgians were installed. From that time to the present patients have come and gone, and from their grateful letters all were more than satisfied with their treatment. Much kindly help outside the detachment has been rendered, and the whole of Bickley has given of its best. Miss Gosselin was unfortunately not able to continue as Quartermaster after April, 1915.

Commandant—MRS. FREDK. BROWN.
Medical Officer—DR. C. LEWIS.
Quartermaster—MRS. CHISHOLM SIMPSON.

Members.—Violet Boreham ; Marguerite Bouvier ; Agnes Allen Brown ; Muriel Clay ; Vera Clay, Stella Clay ; Beatrice Davies, May Fawcett ; Grace Gibson ; Muriel Gosselin ; Marjorie Henderson ; Edith Holloway ; Ethel Jefferson, Jemima Jefferson ; Dorothy Jefferson ; Violet Johns ; Evelyn Lamb, Georgiana Leadbetter ; Vera Livett, Dorothy Lord ; Dorothy Lovell ; Gwendolen Mawe ; Mary McMillan ; Gladys Moore, Violet Nash, Daisy Nash ; Elizabeth Oboussier, Marion Pawley ; Mabel Beresford Pierse, Elizabeth Sandle ; Emily Shipper ; Lily Shipper ; Freda Stacey ; Elizabeth Turpin ; Helen Vallings, Primrose Vallings ; Sophie de Wael ; Jessie Walduck.

Linen Room—Mrs and Miss McMillan

Kitchen Orderlies.—Mesdames Burnie ; Chaldecot, Millar ; Paton, Stenning ; Sydney Smith ; Symington, Misses Badcock (two), Cooper, G and M Cork, Downs, Dutson, Hawkins, Holdron ; Houghton, Humphreys, Lake, Moore, Rowe ; Staples, Stonard ; Walters, White.

KENT 80, FARNBOROUGH. As soon as the present war broke out lectures were started, and the detachment considerably strengthened.

The order to mobilise was received on October 16th; for this the trustees of the Wesleyan Church kindly placed at the disposal of the detachment their church, and within twelve hours a hospital, capable of taking seventeen patients, was ready, entirely equipped by loans and donations from residents in the neighbourhood.

Commandant—MISS B. GREENWAY.
Medical Officer—DR. J. F. DOUSE.
Lady Superintendent—MRS. DURTNELL.
Quartermaster—MISS R. DAVIS.

Members.—Beatrice Blundell; Mabel Challen, Gwen Davis; Phyllis Davis; Ethel Mary Douse; Alice Ellam; Charlotte Hellier; Margaret Ledgar; Elsie March; Mabel Paice; Gladys Plumbridge; Kathleen Shannon; Helen Sharp; Caroline Straker; Lilian Patricia Swan; Constance Swift; Lucie Twitchell; Daisy Vidal; Phyllis West.

KENT 82, WEST WICKHAM, was formed in 1913, after most of the candidates had passed their exams. Classes for lectures, drills, and practical work were held and members went into camp that year at Herne, winning Dr. Yolland's shield against fifteen other detachments.

In August, 1914, preparations for mobilisation were made, and about £350 was guaranteed by the residents in the neighbourhood. Sir Robert Laidlaw generously offered his house at Hayes,

" The Warren," promising £25 per week and the use of five servants.

There are fifty-five beds in the hospital, with an operating theatre, for which Mr. Gurney Preston gave an operating table and two tables for dressings.

The detachment was mobilised on October 14th, and has treated over 250 patients, Belgians and British.

Sir Everard Hambro kindly lent " Hayes Grove " as an additional hospital for twenty patients, supplying the equipment and giving £5 per week towards the upkeep.

Very great credit is due to Miss Gillian Lee-Warner and the Quartermaster for all the work undertaken by them in the earlier stages of the war.

Commandant—MRS. GRIPPER.
Medical Officer—DR. BLAKE.
Lady Superintendent—MISS MAXWELL.
Quartermaster—MRS. E. M. KERSHAW.

Members—Rosa Blake, Helen Butler, Blodwyn Clark, Louis Daws, Alice Farr, Annie Fuller, Mary Katherine Gripper; Patience Gripper, Annie Gussin, Adelaide Hemming; Gertrude Heufrey, Maud Hurnall, Ada Lawrence, Gillian Lee-Warner, Maude Lee-Warner, Grace Lennard, Constance Millim, Elizabeth Orde, Mary Orde, Elsie Preston; Edith Rockwood, Agnes Robertson, Marjory Sherrard; Violet Smith

KENT 84, CRAYFORD, was started in 1912 by Mrs. Butcher of Barnes Cray House.

Drills were held weekly, and, after the outbreak of

war, some of the members worked as probationers at the Livingstone Hospital, Dartford.

On the outbreak of war the detachment made every preparation for opening a hospital, and on October 14th, at 2 a.m., orders for mobilisation were received, with instructions to be ready at 9 a.m.

The two hospitals, i.e. the Parish Hall lent by the Rector and the Friendly Hall and Working Men's Institute lent by the Friendly Society and Working Men's Club, were quickly prepared and the wounded, forty-three Belgians, eventually arrived early on the 16th. Besides the Belgians many of the Territorials from the neighbouring barracks have been treated.

The inhabitants of Crayford have been most kind and willing to help.

Commandant—Miss Evans.
Medical Officer—Dr. J. E. Walker.
Lady Superintendent—Miss Stanley.
Quartermaster—Miss M. Mann.

Members—Grace Baker; Lottie Bond; Joan Carvosso; Esther Clarke; Edith Cooper; Margery Cox; Winifred Cox; Bessie Ferdinand; Grace Hartley; Ethel Letchford; Lena McGregor; Catherine Nicholson, Daisy Powell, Emily Powell; Edith Ranshaw; Ethel Saunders, Mabel Skingley; Annie Smith; Elizabeth Smith.

KENT 86, BECKENHAM. In December, 1912, a meeting was held to explain the aims and methods of the Red Cross V.A.D. Names were enrolled and Kent No. 86 was formed. Lectures were arranged, examinations held, and members had the advantage of three weeks' training at Marylebone and Paddington Infirmaries.

In a short time the detachment became so large that it was split and Kent 96 was formed. The detachments did useful practical work at Rolvenden Camp on the eve of the outbreak of war, when working parties were at once organised and further training secured at the Cottage Hospital. Christ Church Schools were lent by the vicar, the Rev. Harrington Lees, and when, on October 13th, the detachments were suddenly mobilised at 2 a.m., it remained only to clear the schools and equip them as a hospital. This was done in a few hours. The hospital contains two wards, capable of holding forty-five patients, two isolation rooms, and a well-equipped operating theatre with a complete X-ray apparatus. One hundred and sixty-nine patients have passed through the wards.

The inhabitants of Beckenham have been most generous in their help. The hospital has the use of fourteen private motor-cars, and these are each on duty once a fortnight.

Commandant—Mrs. Neame.
Medical Officer—Dr. Strickland.
Lady Superintendent—Miss Savory.
Quartermaster—Miss J. Stenning.

Members—Beatrice Adams; Esme Anderson; Mildred Bowyer; Muriel Cardross-Grant, Merlo Cow; Georgina Creo, Evelyn Dermer; Freda Dermer; Gladys Dermer; Sybil

Dunlop; Florence Eden; Alice Mary Furze; Eva Gallie; Edith Lee Gibberd; Dorothy Giddings; Rosa Grieg; Helena Harrison; Agatha Hawthorne; Ethel Hawthorne, Marion Hudson, Frances Hudson; Nesta Inglis; Doris Jones; Hilda Lazenby; Mary Litchfield; Winnie Manger; Violet Margaret Mather, Eirene Mather, Winnie Mather; — Maynard; Hilda Mitchell; Eva Morley; — Oakes; Marjory Paterson; Poppy Paterson; Cicely Pattisson; Madge Pattisson, Lucy Price, Edith Robinson; Eleanor Sharpe; Emily Stenning, Ellen Sterling, Mary Eanswyth Tolhurst; Mary Trimmer; Eveline Young, Mesdames Clarke, Ginn, Kent, Privit, Treggis, Wilson.

KENT 88, EDENBRIDGE. When it became apparent early in the war that all the accommodation possible would be required it was found that there was no building in Edenbridge large enough for a hospital. But so eager were Kent 88 to put into practice the training they had so strenuously acquired that the difficulty was overcome by opening three hospitals, each with accommodation for ten patients:

1. Church House, generously offered rent free.

2. Eden Hall, the home of the present Commandant.

3. Marlpit Hill Men's Institute.

On mobilisation at midnight on October 14th everything was quickly got ready and at eleven o'clock the following morning the first convoy arrived. To the surprise of the detachment the wounded proved to be Belgians, but the language difficulty was quickly overcome.

Offers of help and gifts poured into the hospital. By Christmas the numbers of patients had considerably dwindled, and these were concentrated at Eden Hall.

Whilst waiting for the next convoy a large empty house, Marlpit Court, lent by Mr. Edwards, has been secured and furnished as a hospital with twenty beds, in place of Marlpit Hill and Church House. Splendid work was put in at the outset by Dr. and Mrs. Hubbard, and it was with great regret that the detachment lost their devoted service in November, 1914, consequent upon Dr. Hubbard's severe illness.

Commandant—COUNTESS RICCARDI-CUBITT.
Medical Officers—
DR. SCOTT, DR. PENNELL, DR. NEWINGTON.
Lady Superintendent—NURSE GIDDINS.
Quartermaster—MISS AKERMAN.

Members.—Eva Akerman ; Norah Akerman, Dorothy Barnes ; Catherine Chapman, Kate Cheal ; May Churches ; Mary Coleman ; Susan Cross ; Theodora Cubitt, Vera Cubitt ; Rowena Curtice, Mary Eeles ; Gertrude Forde ; Kathleen Finn Keley ; Hannah Giddins ; Ethel Goffin ; Florence Hammond ; Nellie Harding, Lillias Hayward, Annie Hubbard, Amelia Hutchinson, Lilian Kelsey ; Constance Knight ; Charis Locket, Lilias Locket, Marjorie Locket ; Mary Lovel, Emma Masters, Coralie Meade-Waldo, Alice Miles, Clara Miller ; Caroline Norman ; Kate Oliver, Mary Pullinger, Fido Riccardi-Cubitt ; Violet Seal ; Isabel Soutter, Martha Staff, Christina Tatnall, Dorothy Treadwell, Marjorie Treadwell, Dorothy West, Ellen West.

KENT 90, HERNE BAY, first came into being in 1913. On the outbreak of hostilities the Dence Trust kindly offered the use of Downs Park College at Herne Bay for the whole period of the war. The hospital was throughout equipped by friends in the neighbourhood.

The detachment was mobilised on October 14th and a week later some of the beds were occupied by wounded Belgians. Since then relays, totalling about sixty patients, have passed through the hospital.

All the work of the hospital is voluntary, and the kitchen staff under Mrs. Lloyd and Miss Grey is particularly efficient.

Commandant—MRS. OPENSHAW.
Medical Officer—DR. FENCULHET.
Lady Superintendent—MRS. CUNNYNGHAME.
Quartermaster—MRS. THURNHAM.

Members.—Mary Bass; Jessie Bawcomb; Violet Browne; Alice Rose Campbell; Phyllis Channing; Gwendolin Chapman; Lois Cremer; Edith Grey; Agnes Hunter; Elsie Iggulden; Madge Iggulden; Dorothy Lang Sims; Ethel Lloyd; Olive McDougall, Hilda Meyer; Mary Mills; Ursula Osmond; Evelyn Paterson; Ivy Smith; Mary Swinford; Mabel Wacher; Mary Whistler; Elsie White.

KENT 92, GRAVESEND. On the outbreak of war this detachment, with Kent 16 and 42, commenced to collect equipment and money, and an offer was received from Messrs. W. G. and A. W. Fletcher, the owners, of the building formerly used as the

New Thames Yacht Club. On mobilisation the members, assisted by Kent 16, quickly prepared the building as a hospital, and on October 15th, 1914, fifty-eight wounded Belgians were received.

Dr. Dismorr was the first medical officer, but increasing private practice compelled his retirement, and the present doctor was appointed, together with the honorary surgeon, Dr. S. M. Lawrence.

Miss Schofield took the position of Matron temporarily, but transferred to the Cobham Hospital. The present Matron, Miss E. M. Tarrant, has had experience in Australia, and has been in charge of more than one hospital. Due to her exertions is the operating theatre, subscribed for by members and their friends. Grateful thanks are due for the ready support given by all in the district. Up to date 224 cases have been treated. Sir Gilbert and Lady Parker take great interest in the welfare of the detachments, and have rendered valuable assistance.

Commandant—MRS. GADD.
Medical Officer—DR. F. MAINWARING HUGHES.
Hon. Surgeon—DR. S. M. LAWRENCE.
Lady Superintendent—MRS. M. TAYLOR.
Quartermaster—MISS M. F. HOYLE.

Members—Edith Acott, Amy Agnew; Emily Allen; Gladys Allen, Blanche Avenell, Madeline Bevis, Irene Blake, Dorothy Broadwood; Mary Broadwood; Gladys Brown,

M

Miss Calvert; Antoinette Crook; Lilian Dickens; Bertha Dunstall; Elizabeth Durrant; Dorothy Evans; Margery Fox; Edith Franklyn; Frances Harvey; Ruby Herring; Gladys Hickmott; Betty Holderness; Margaret Horrigan; Eva Howes; Caroline Johnson; Doris Keeley; Mary Limington; Eleanor Luck, Grace Luck; Agnes Maplesden; Annie Sandford; Sarah Sandford; Isabella Schofield; Kathleen Shepherd; Mabel Starkey; M. K. Tristram; Agnes Veevers; Eleanor Warlters; Gertrude Warren; Miss Willoughby; Freda Winder.

KENT 94, TUNBRIDGE WELLS, was organised in 1913. From the first much invaluable help was received from doctors and nurses in the town, who gave lectures and superintended practices.

In August, 1914, working parties were organised, advanced lectures held, and several members were allowed to work in two of the local hospitals.

Mr. Harris Gastrell generously offered his house, West Hall, as a hospital for fifty cases, and this was furnished and equipped entirely by local residents.

At 5 a.m. on October 14th mobilisation orders were received, and at 9.30 a.m. the first contingent of wounded Belgians was received, St. John Ambulance then acting as bearers.

Early in December wounded English began to arrive.

At the request of the R.A.M.C. officers in the

town fourteen beds were reserved for local troops, and these have been kept occupied.

Commandant—Miss V. M. Moore.
Medical Officers—
Drs. G. T. Watson, R. A. Walter, B. F. B Manser.
Lady Superintendent—Miss P. Dunster.
Quartermaster—Mrs. Faulkner.

Members.—Evelyn Barnes ; Janet Bell ; Kate Bell ; Doris Candy ; Aileen Faulkner ; Hope Glover , Monica Handley ; Edith Happell , Kathleen Hardy ; Rita Hay ; Maude Higginson ; Grace O'Bryen Hodge ; Marjorie O'Bryen Hodge ; Janet Hull ; Dorothy Hyde ; Winifred Jones ; Elsie Kerr ; Laura King , Mildred Knott ; Margaret Layard ; Margaret Logan ; Carol Lowry ; Annette Maingay ; Olive Manser ; Grace Morley , Amy Murdoch ; Agnes Nix ; Marguerite Rainier ; Lucy Ranking ; Cherry Robbins ; Margaret Seymour ; Marjorie Snelgrove , Irene Sutton ; Alice Sword ; Winifred Sykes , Dora Symes ; Edith Symes ; Lynette Tewson , Catherine Warmington ; Ada Webb ; Agnes Wilkinson.

Kent 96, Beckenham, was formed from Kent 86 in 1913 and co-operated with that detachment in all the preparations for Red Cross work and in opening and working Christ Church Hospital. Dr. Ramsbotham, the then Commandant, rendered invaluable assistance, together with Mrs. Ramsbotham, and it was with great regret that the detachment lost their services when both were accepted for active work at the front.

Kelsey Cottage, generously lent by Mr. Preston, was opened in November as the Kelsey Auxiliary

Red Cross Hospital, where fifty-one patients can be treated. Miss Constance Sharpe, who took over the duties of Commandant from Dr. Ramsbotham, also had most unfortunately to give up duty, when Mrs. Fisher took charge. Lighter cases are usually received at Kelsey, and very marked progress is soon reported. A great deal of the comfort of the hospital is due to the efficient voluntary service rendered by those who so kindly undertake the cleaning of the house. After much excellent and self-denying labour Mrs. Fisher had, for private reasons, to relinquish the command in May, 1915, when the present officer was appointed.

Commandant—MRS. NICHOLSON.
Quartermaster—MISS OLIVE LEWER.

Members.—Muriel Anns ; Joyce Baker ; Muriel Bowden ; Marjory Brown ; Marion Carpenter ; Barbara Castell ; Phyllis Castell ; Evelyn Challenger ; Eileen Clarke ; Grace Collier ; Margaret Ewins ; Lucrece Fiddes ; Elizabeth Greig ; Mary Hooper ; Sybil Leighton ; L. Mather ; Mabel Mather ; Helen Moses ; Marjorie Neame ; Grace Nicholson ; Florence Petley ; Dora Reynolds ; Constance Sharpe ; Nancy Stainbank ; Rosalind Stinson ; Dorothy Tremel ; May Tremel ; Katherine Wade ; Margaret Ward ; Annie Wedekind ; Hilda Wedekind ; Lily Wedekind ; Catherine Whittington ; Lilian Wright.

KENT 98, SOUTHBOROUGH, was registered in 1913 as the result of a meeting held at the Victoria Hall, Southborough, for the purpose of forming a

Red Cross detachment. On October 14th, 1914, the detachment was mobilised, and on the 21st the Victoria Hall, lent by the District Council, was opened as a hospital.

At the beginning of the war a guarantee fund was started and liberally responded to, and the inhabitants have freely given and lent equipment for the hospital, also rendering gratuitous service whenever required.

Commandant—LADY SALOMONS.
Medical Officers—DRS. BAYFIELD AND REYNOLDS.
Lady Superintendent—MISS ASKWITH.
Quartermaster—MISS SALOMONS.

Members—Edith Burr; Alice Fartlung; Alethea Kirby; Florence Leigh-Sarney, Ada Marshall, Lottie Martin; Lucy Martin; Beatrice Newman, Annie Seale; Amy Stunt.

KENT 100, CANTERBURY, took charge of Abbotts Barton Hospital, kindly lent by Mr. Bennett Goldney, M.P., whose residence it is. It contains forty beds for patients, and the Red Cross committee for Canterbury supplies any amounts needed over and above the War Office grant. The trained sisters gave their services, whilst the cook took half wages only, but after three months the committee decided that such sacrifice was not necessary on the part of these ladies. Three hundred patients have been cared for since October 4th, seventy-two of these being Belgians. The medical officer has charge of the Canterbury section transport.

Commandant—Miss Frances Carnegie Wemyss.
Medical Officer—Dr. R. J. Ferguson.
Quartermaster—Miss M. R. Williamson.

Members —Ida Baker ; Madeline Bates ; Mabel Beatson ; Winifred Beatson ; Lily Bird ; Agnes Bousfield ; Geraldine Clarke ; Mildred Clarke ; Finovola Cordy-Simpson ; Violet Cremer ; Catherine Dyneley ; Bertha Evans ; Carol Frend ; Camilla Frend ; Dorothy Gilham ; Violet Countess of Guilford ; Ethel Hankin ; Kathleen Hilton ; Annie Kay ; Janet Malden ; Margaret Marshall ; Helen Mills ; Beatrice Moore ; Ursula Morris ; Alice Murton ; Irene Oldham ; Audrey Patterson , Myrtle Stuart , Mary Trueman , Beryl Tuke ; Joan Wacher.

Kent 102, Biddenden. The first interest in V.A.D. work was aroused in 1909 at a meeting at Hemsted Park called by Cicely Countess of Cranbrook, and the detachment was registered in 1914. Mobilisation orders were received on October 14th, and a small hospital was opened in the village Institute, sympathisers in Biddenden generously helping with equipment, etc.

Commandant—Mrs. C. Hall.
Medical Officer—Dr. Boyce.
Lady Superintendent—Sister J. Stone.
Quartermaster—Mrs. Phillip Jones.

Members —Louisa Austen ; Ellen Avory ; Augusta Boyce ; Helen Bradshaw ; Helen Mary Dormer ; Gertrude Edwards ; Elsie Elliott , Emily Giin , Alice Jones ; Gladys Pinyon ; Lydia Stapley , Edythe Stuart ; Mary Tassell ; Eva Thirkell ; Muriel Todd-Naylor , Alice Watts ; May Witherden.

Ada Wise, unable to serve, gives assistance with laundry work.

KENT 104 AND 106. Strood and Frindsbury Hospital consists of two neighbouring buildings, organised by Dr. G. A. Skinner. The owners granted the buildings free of charge, and the Council freed them also from rates and taxes. Kent 126 works in conjunction with these two detachments, and the first patients were received on September 3rd, 1914. Since that date four hundred patients have passed through the hospitals, and a larger number of local troops have been treated as out-patients. An up-to-date operating theatre has been fully equipped, and the detachments possess their own motor ambulance and dispensary. The beds are now to be increased to 130. Dr. Skinner, Assistant County Director, No. 2 Division, has charge of the distribution of the wounded when the convoys arrive at the railway station.

Commandants—
MISS M. SKINNER, MRS. SKINNER.
Medical Officer—
DR. SKINNER.
Lady Superintendents—
MRS. POCOCK, MRS. BLANEY.
Quartermasters—
MRS. IRELAND, MRS. H. B. CLARKE, MRS. ELLIOTT.

Members—Elizabeth Brain, Emily Bunyard, Nellie Cooper; Lena Homewood, Violet Hysted, Nellie Jackson; Bertha Leney Sarah Millard, Dorothy Parker; Clara Robson; Maria Thatcher

KENT 108, ORPINGTON. Due to the exertions

of the Quartermaster and of the members of the detachment who had canvassed the district for promises of equipment, a hospital, containing thirty beds, was quickly made ready at the village Hall when mobilisation orders were received on October 14th, 1914. Wounded Belgians were soon installed. Another party was landed at St. Mary Cray, and, thanks to the generosity of the Misses Lyster, who placed their schoolhouse at the disposal of the detachment, a temporary hospital of twenty-five beds was established. A week later these patients were transferred to the Institute, St. Mary Cray, equipped by E. H. Joynson, Esq. This hospital was closed when the patients were convalescent, and all cases are now treated at Orpington. An operating theatre is being installed.

E. Rock Carling, F.R.C.S., of Harley Street, and W. Ironside Bruce act as Hon. Consulting Surgeons.

Commandant and Medical Officer—
DR. TENNYSON SMITH.
*Assistant Medical Officer—*DR. THOMAS BAILEY.
*Lady Superintendent—*MRS. TENNYSON SMITH.
*Quartermaster—*MISS GAMMON.

Members.—Winifred Bickmore ; Amy Crosse ; Virginie Dolan ; Beatrice Fooks ; Mabel Greenwood ; Joyce Harrild ; Marjorie Harrild ; Vera Harrild ; Isabel Hoar, Irene Holroyd, Amy Howard ; Hilda Larmarque ; Eliza Lewis ; Winifred Miller-Hallett, Lilian Morris ; Mabel Philips ; Ethel Simpson ; Mabel Smith ; Nora Symons ; Irene Temperley ; Hilda Townsend ; Miriam Townsend ; Winifred Tremame ; Ethel Tyrer ; Mildred Virtue ; Mary Waring ; Marjorie Wisely ; Hirel Wright.

KENT 110 AND 112, ABBEY WOOD. The Belvedere women's detachments were raised on the outbreak of war by Mrs. Butcher and family. Lectures were at once started, and the members met daily for practice.

Mobilisation orders were received at 2 a.m. on October 14th, 1914. The two Quartermasters at once called up the detachments. Six a.m. saw the members hard at work cleaning and preparing their temporary hospital—" Shornells "—the residence of the late Mr. Hudson Church, kindly lent by his four daughters. Equipment, previously promised by the residents, was collected, and by the afternoon the hospital was complete. Belgians were the first patients to be received, but these have all been discharged, the present occupants being British soldiers.

The hospital has been almost entirely equipped by gifts and loans from residents in the district, and is indebted, both financially and for personal service, to Mrs. Callender of Abbey Wood.

Commandants—
MISS BUTCHER AND MRS. BUTCHER.
Medical Officer—DR. BARRY CANE.
Lady Superintendent—MISS M. SLATTERY.
Quartermasters—
MISS V. BUTCHER AND MISS MAY BUTCHER

Members — Ethel Abbott; Ruby Abbott; Florence Baddeley; Irene M. Bayley, Dora Blyth; Alice J. Cane; Gertrude W Cane, Dorothy Cornish; Ruth Cowley, Dorothy Garrett;

Clara L. Hartwright; Alice M. Knight; Edith Lester; Muriel Lumley; Ellen L. Lynde; Lydia Munden; Ethel M. Palmer; Blanche Scarlett; Ailsie Griffith Searight; Eileen Searight; Ailsie Lilian Searight; Madeline Sidley; Doris Sidley; Annie Walker, Mary E. J. Willard; Norah Wright.

BELVEDERE, Kent 112

Members.—Georgette Adam; Letty Bedwell; Mary E. Biggs; Dorothy Billington; Dorothy M Blyth; Beryl Butcher; Grace Chapman; Elsie Charlesworth; M. Edith Darken; Kate Eastwood; E. Mary Flack, Emily E. French; Edith M Fullaway; Edith M. Gloyn; Gertrude Hayward, Katie Hayward, Mabel Herbert; Maude Hooker; Florence F. C Lyster; Frances Marshall; Gwendoline E Masson; Sarah Pooler; Ellen Rider, Florence E. Simms; Florence Simms; Annie Whitmore.

KENT 114, SHOREHAM. The small but very pleasant hospital is at Myrtle College, and has accommodation for seven patients. Much useful work has been done by this detachment, which was previously under the command of Mrs. Wilmot.

Commandant—MISS GWENDOLEN MADGE.
Medical Officer—DR. PASSMORE.
Lady Superintendent—MRS. GEORGE BELL.
Quartermaster—MISS COHEN.

Members.—Annie Ansell; Alice Bell; Elizabeth Bowers; Alice Chapman; Ellen Clark, Jacobina Clark; Fanny Collins, Annie Gooding; Carol Greenwood; Gwendolen Greenwood; Bertine Gregory; Phœbe Gregory; Margaret Madge; Gladys Randall; Isobel Scott; Sarah Steane; Kate Taylor.

KENT 116, DARTFORD, was initiated at a meeting called by Mr. F. J. Pile, who was appointed the first Commandant, with Mrs. A. H. Botten as

Quartermaster. Weekly drills were well attended, and lectures were given by Miss Stanley.

On October 14th, 1914, the detachment was mobilised, and the Wesley Hall was fitted up as a hospital. The equipment was generously given or lent by the townspeople. Credit is due to Mr. C. J. Mansford, of the Dartford Grammar School, for much of the preliminary work. Owing to structural alterations becoming necessary this hospital had to be closed, and on November 13th "Heath Close" was taken over and the equipment transferred. This hospital has proved most useful for the reception of sick soldiers stationed in the district.

A change of officers took place in January, the present Commandant being appointed, with Mrs. Annie Read and subsequently Mrs. Black as Quartermaster. Mr. F. J. Pile took over the important transport duties for Dartford section, and became Honorary Commandant to this detachment.

Commandant—MRS. C. M. REED.
Medical Officer—DR. GRAHAM ROBERTSON.
Lady Superintendent—NURSE CLIFF.
Quartermaster—MRS. BLACK.

Members —Mrs. Abbey ; Miss Abbey ; Alice Adams ; Gladys Allen ; Ada Basham ; May Brow, R. Burgess ; Clara Cleveland, A Coles, May Cooper ; Gladys Crawter ; H. Draper, M. Edgecumbe, Emily Fairbrass ; May Gore-Brown, Lucy Heiseman ; Mrs Lyon ; Rosina McKney ; N E Pott ; May Walker, Lelia Whiting ; Mrs. Wood.

KENT 118, GREENHITHE. On the outbreak of war a women's Red Cross detachment was formed, and on mobilisation Ingress Abbey was equipped and staffed by private generosity, under the Chatham Military Hospital, with accommodation for sixty beds, in the care of a fully trained matron, six sisters and a house surgeon.

Commandant—MRS. SYDNEY ALLNUTT.
Medical Officer—DR. RICHMOND.
Lady Superintendent—MRS. RICHMOND.
Quartermaster—MISS M. WATSON.

Members.—Alice Ames; Jessie Barnes; Ethel Bartrum; Elizabeth Bridger; Nellie Burt; Florence Chatfield; Gertrude Davis; Sarah Dyble; Elizabeth Ellis, Grace Hardy; Rose Ireland; Maud Kernick; Jessie Langston; Rhoda Lee; Hettie Lockyer; Margaret Mackenzie; Elizabeth Newnham; Agnes Oakes; Sylvia Richmond; Kate Showell; Dorothy Smith; Lizzie Wheatley; Kate Wood; Agnes Woodcock.

KENT 120, HASTINGS. The Hospital of St. John of Jerusalem had its beginning in August, 1914, at the outbreak of war, when all members were summoned to prepare themselves for the work before them and classes were held every night.

On mobilisation a house in the centre of the town was kindly lent by Mrs. Stubbs and rapidly transformed into a V.A.D. hospital by the volunteer nurses. Belgian wounded arrived on October 13th, and in January the first convoy of English soldiers was received. At this time another house was offered by Mr. Parks, bringing the accommodation up to fifty beds.

Thirty members are available for duty under the supervision of two fully trained sisters and two certificated nurses. Dr. Morgan, the first Commandant, undertook military service soon after the outbreak of war, and the present officer carried on the detachment.

A considerable sum of money is collected weekly to supplement the War Office grant, and equipment has been freely lent and given.

The girl guides give invaluable help as doorporters.

Hastings was specially attached to the Kent V.A.D.

Commandant—DR. GEORGE LOCKE.
Medical Officer—DR. JAMES D. HESSEY.
Lady Superintendent—MISS FLORENCE VANSTONE.
Quartermaster—MISS WINIFRED C. COXETER.
Pharmacist—MARY ALICE LOBLEY.

Members.—Minnie Bates; Florence Gertrude Begbie; Ada Mary Benyon-Winser, Ethel Blackman; Lizzie Blomfield; Alice Louise Bowers, Georgina Bruce; Amy Buckett; Frances Jessie Clarke; Margaret Dorothy Coxeter; Marjorie Eldridge; Georgia Finger, Gertrude Mary Fowell; Margaret Hill; Celia Hinks; Louise Inkpen; Edith Jane Larcombe; Lily Ransom, Nellie Rowland, Susan Selwood, Winifred Skinner; Ann Mary Viner, Rosetta Walther, Ethel Mary Watt; Edith Mary Wicks, Emilie Wilshin.

KENT 122, GOUDHURST. At the beginning of the war the detachment was formed and classes were organised. The Commandant offered his house, "Lidwells," as a hospital, and money and equipment were promised by local residents. Two trained nurses offered their services upon mobilisation, which took place in May, 1915.

Twenty beds are provided and are now kept well occupied in this very pleasant and fully-equipped hospital.

Commandant—REV. H. P. FITZ GERALD.
Medical Officer—SURGEON LT.-COL. COLLINGRIDGE.
Lady Superintendent—MRS. FITZ GERALD.
Quartermaster—MISS RAIKES.

Members.—Editha Barry; Margaret Constance Burgess; Ruby Burgess; Norah Burke; Annie Calcutt, Margaret Cheeseman, Ada Mary Clemetson; Florence Annie Mary Cole; Elsie Collingridge; Marian Louisa Crump; Frances Anne Davis; Frances Mary Davis; Ida Davis; Rosa Maud Gouldthorpe; Sarah Elizabeth Haines; Maud Emily Jenner; Kate Johnson; Clarice Kendon; Ianthe Kershaw; Doris Large; Mabel Large; Kathleen Emily Maude; Florence Morley; Adelaide Nicolson; Violet Noakes; Margaret Penny; Aileen Rivett-Carnac; Elizabeth Smith; Ellice Fletcher Smith; Ellen Louisa Southam; Marjorie Waters; Lily Elizabeth Wickham; Norah Wickham.

KENT 124, DOVER, undertakes the duty of assisting with refreshment at the disembarkation of the wounded when convoys arrive at the Pier Head, and is doing much quietly useful work.

Commandant—MRS. E. G. WYNNE.

KENT 126, STROOD, is working in conjunction with detachments 104 and 106 at the Strood Hospital, rendering the greatest possible assistance.

Commandant—MISS O. P. HAGGARD.
Medical Officer—DR. SKINNER.
Lady Superintendent—MISS HEWSON.
Quartermaster—MRS. ELLIOT.

Members—Alice Allen, Mabel Allen; Maud Bigge, Grace Fielder; Elsie Larcombe; Clare Latham; Nellie May; Fanny Myhill; Mildred Newson; Mary Sayer.

KENT 128, ASH. In August, 1914, the inhabitants of Ash were asked by Dr. McCall-Smith to lend the village hall as a hospital, and the trustees gave their consent. On October 25th the detachment was mobilised; the thirty members quickly prepared the hall with twenty beds, and in less than two hours twenty wounded Belgians were installed. Since January British soldiers have been cared for, many operations having been successfully performed.

Commandant—MRS. McCALL-SMITH.
Medical Officer—DR. McCALL-SMITH.
Lady Superintendent—MISS M. HARRISON.
Quartermaster—MRS H. WILSON.

Members—Thelma Bicknell, May Buley, Mary Chandler, Rosa Gardner, Connie Harden, Doris Harrison; Edith Herbert, Annie Jacobs; Amy Jenner, Dora Jenner, Fonnie Mackenzie, Dulcie Macmeiken, Mabel Maxted; Kathie Miles, Stella Parker; Dorothy Petley; Bessy Quested, Ruby Streeter, Miss Westmorland

KENT 130, BEXLEY. To Mrs. Burridge, Vice-President of Kent 130, and the Committee, is due the credit of this detachment being formed, and on the declaration of war the present Commandant was able to bring the detachment up to full strength.

Mobilisation orders were received on October 14th at 10.30 a.m., when the members took charge of "Gardenhurst," lent by Mrs. Arthur Barrett. The house had stood empty for eight years, so that the detachment had very hard work to do in preparing the place as a hospital. The local residents were most generous in providing equipment and funds.

Commandant—MRS. N. CHRISTOPHERSON.
Medical Officer—DR. J. E. WALKER.
Lady Superintendent—NURSE A. M. BUNCE.
Quartermaster—MRS. R. T. GUMBLETON.

Members —Hilda Aldis ; Minnie Baker ; Lucy Brown ; Daisie Burridge ; Constance Cutcliffe ; Priscilla Escombe ; Adeline Footitt , Madeline Friswell ; Helena Gough ; Maud Hamilton ; Rachel Howe ; Marjorie Hudson ; Ada Kennard ; Mary Loxley ; Alice Lucas ; Clare Lucas ; Alice Radford ; Winifred Rubeck ; Suzan Sewell ; Mary Simon ; Maud Simonds ; Ethel Stimson ; Kathleen Upton ; Marjorie Vesey-Holt ; Eveline Webb ; Elsie Whalley , Christabel Whitehead ; Joan Whitehead.

KENT 132, SYDENHAM, is ready to take twenty patients, when called upon, at "Brooklyn,"

Sydenham; and fifteen British soldiers are now being cared for at this pleasant hospital.

Commandant—Miss Ada Bennett.
Medical Officer—Dr. Umney.
Lady Superintendent—Nurse Shand.
Quartermaster—Miss Irene Carter.

Members —Vera Alabaster; Maud Alston; Ethel Badcock; Mabel Bellamy, Lottie Bennett; Phyllis Boxall; Nellie Brigg; Dora Brookes; Enid Clarke-Williams; Claire de Baerdemaecker; Olive de Pury; Ruby de Pury; May Faux; Agnes Gaman, Ethel George; Phyllis Gooch; Bertha Grose; Gertrude Johnston; Gladys Johnston; Glenda Jolly; Beatrice Jones; Stephanie Langmead; Sibyl Owsley; Ethel Partridge; Elsie Pryce; Dorothy Pynegar; Winifred Selby; Amy Shackleton; Millie Stedman; Dora Sturman; Muriel Umney; Helen Waterson.

Kent 134, Lenham, is a compact detachment fully prepared to take up duty at Lenham and Harrietsham. All arrangements are complete, and eighteen patients are installed.

Commandant and Medical Officer—
Dr. Temperley Grey.
Lady Superintendent—Miss Plowman.
Quartermaster—Mrs. H. M. Campbell.

Members —Ellen L S Bensted; Elizabeth Jane Broad; Constance Campbell, Clarissa Clark; Ethel Clark, Nellie Clark. Annie Collins; Emma Collins, Adeline Day; Bertha Grey; Nellie Kitchin, Edith Kortright, Mary Lucy, Norah Maylam; Fanny L. Norris, Gladys Shayer, Margaret Woolley.

N

KENT 136, NEW ROMNEY, has not yet been mobilised, but is fully prepared for any emergency.

Commandant—MISS MAUD COBB.
Medical Officers—
DR. MOSSOP, DR. HICK.
Quartermaster—MRS. H. G. SOUTH.

Members.—Alice Anderson ; Amy Anderson ; Evelyn Anderson ; Kathleen Bannon, Elizabeth Campbell, Frances de Luze ; Marie de Luze ; Marguerete Ellis ; Florence Fagg ; Alice Finn-Kelsey ; Emily Heard ; Ethel Hobbs, Evelyn Hobbs ; Ellinor Howes, Elsie Kennett ; Ethel Knight ; Maud Mossop ; Louie Murray ; Edith Palmer ; Rosa Pearson ; Kathleen Pritchard ; Rosa Pritchard ; Effie Ringland ; Edith Tuffield ; Annie Vidgen.

KENT 138, WHITSTABLE, have not yet the opportunity of utilising their experience, but will render a very good account of themselves when called upon. Eleven are giving their services at the Military Hospital.

Commandant—MISS G. CAMPBELL.
Medical Officer—DR. C. ETHERIDGE.
Quartermaster—MISS POOLE.

Members—Dorothy Beard ; Florence Brightman ; Dorothy Carson ; Mabel Collings ; Clara Cook, Beatrice Couper ; Frances Davis ; Maude Davis ; Ethel Dorman ; Mary Etheridge ; Ethel Fortesque ; Emmeline Gann ; Dorothy Gill ; Mabel Hayward ; Gladys Horden ; Adela Jones ; Mabel Kirkby ; Ivy Kingston, Philamena MacIntyre ; Romola McKenzie ; Hilda Mitchell ; Amelia Page ; Mina Pout ; Mary Powell ; Annie Rigden ; May Rushworth ; Antonia Scrymgeour ; Mabel Ware ; Ellen Wood.

KENT 140, FAVERSHAM, was formed from the nursing division in October, 1914, and mobilised at once. A large empty house, "The Mount," Faversham, was offered rent free by the executors of the late Mr. Percy Neame and the neighbourhood was canvassed for promises of equipment, etc. Friends responded willingly, with the result that very little had to be bought. The hospital was opened on November 18th with fifty-two beds. One hundred and forty patients have passed through, including men from the Front and from local troops.

Many contributions have been received.

The doctors and trained nurses are all voluntary workers, the cooking is managed by ladies, and cars are freely lent for transport work.

Commandant—MRS. ALEXANDER.

Medical Officer—DR. G. J. EVERS.

Lady Superintendent—MRS. WITHERS.

Quartermaster—MISS F. K. CROSSE.

Members—Dorothy Alexander ; Muriel Alexander ; Eva Amos , Louisa Amos, Margaret Amos, Olive Amos; Alice Andrews ; Frieda Barnett; Annie Boorman ; Edith Brown; Ethel Buffee, Jessie Bushell, Lily Cook, Minnie Cook; Mrs. Flossie Cornfoot , Miss Flossie Cornfoot ; Molly Cotterill ; Frances Crosse , Bertha Dengate ; Marion Dunn , Dora Edwards , Emily Ellis , Annie Evers , Gladys Filmer , Edith Gillett , Lizzie Gubbins ; Flossie Hawkins ; Eunice Holder , Gwen Jenkins , Lizzie Johnson , Eleanor Lyons , Nellie Miller , Ethel Murton , Margaret Neame , Maud Neame , Dorothy Nunns, Frances Packham , Nellie Packham , Hilda Roberson , Norah Roberson , Violet Roberson ; Betty Robins , Ethel Seward , Louisa Sherwood , Alice Smith , Mildred Steed , Elsie Vinson ; Nellie Williams ; Nellie Wise

KENT 142, WALMER, was formed in August, 1914. On mobilisation the services of the detachment were given to Kent 22, with whom they have worked at St. Anselm's, Walmer. Three members have been lent to the temporary hospital attached to Kent 40, Deal.

Commandant—MISS D. M. LAPAGE.
Medical Officer—DR. MASON.
Lady Superintendent—MRS. LLOYD.
Quartermaster—MISS P. LLOYD.
Pharmacist—MISS J. THOMAS.

Members.—Annie Balchin ; Annie Mary Bass ; Marian Bayly ; Mabel Blogg ; Marjorie Blogg ; Edith Ellen Bowles ; Evelyn Coast ; Evelyn Denne ; Grace Fletcher ; Ada Green ; Lilian Locke ; Muriel Lucas ; Rose Moggridge ; Beatrice Patterson ; Margaret Patterson ; Ena Mary Russell ; Annie Ryder ; Mildred Slaughter ; Gertrude Stevens ; Eva Nellie Todman ; Hilda Mary Todman.

KENT 144, WOODCHURCH, was initiated at a meeting held in the village school, a committee was formed, and offers of financial help towards opening a hospital were made, Mrs. Somerset Webb acting as treasurer ; also offers of equipment and service have been received.

Unfortunately, owing to the much-regretted death of the Medical Officer, Dr. Cape Doughty, and the consequent resignation of his widow as Commandant, the detachment was placed in the difficulty of losing its principal officers. The posts have been filled as follows :—

Commandant—MRS. BOURNE.
Medical Officer—DR. W. DREW MITCHELL.
Lady Superintendent—MRS. A. TANTON.
Quartermaster—MISS B. M. HARPUR.

Members.—Elizabeth Arthur ; Annie Baker ; Edith Bourne ; Mabel Bourne ; Violet Catchpole ; Eva Collick ; Maud Cottar ; Margery Doughty ; Mabel George ; Jessie Huntley ; Elsie Johnston ; Jane Marshall ; Elsie Milton ; Dorothy Tanton ; Sarah Vincett.

KENT 146, BROADSTAIRS, was mobilised on October 14th, with some fifty voluntary workers.

The detachment has charge of two hospitals at Broadstairs which are run in conjunction. " Fairfield," the residence of Norman Craig, Esq., M.P., and lent by him for the purpose of a Red Cross Hospital with forty beds and a small operating theatre ; also " Roseneath," lent by the Committee of the Jacob Memorial Home with thirty beds.

Various gifts have been received from residents in the locality. Dr. Brightman has also to perform the onerous duties of Joint Assistant County Director for No. 7 Division of Kent.

Commandant—MRS. BRIGHTMAN.
Medical Officers—
DRS. AYTOUN, BRIGHTMAN, PINNIGER, RAVEN, ROBINS.
Dentist—M. C. REED.
Lady Superintendent—MISS D. MUIR.
Quartermaster—MISS R. MASKS.

Members.—Dorothy Alfreo ; Florence Allen ; Muriel Andrews ; May Athawes, Enid Athawes ; Gertrude Austin ; Doris

Bartrum; Frances Bromfield; Phyllis Brightman; Myrtle Broadhead; Emily Burnham; Louisa Burnham; Eva Bush; Marjorie Bush; Rosa Bush; Jessie Caldwell; Jean Caird; Constance Chamberlain; May Chapple; Christine Church; Esther Cornock; Mabel Dames; May Dacres; Adelaide Daniels; Jessie Davis; Joy Davis; Molly Davis; Carol Denton; Dorcas Denton; Fanny Denton; Maud Dennant; Lilian Elsworthy; Clara Eveling; Mona Farrar; Helen Fiske; Dorothy Forster; Kathleen Foster; Margaret Goodey; Marjorie Gullick; Jennie Hall; Bessie Halfnight; Agnes Harrison; Grace Hickie; Gertrude Inglis; Meta Iles; Eva Inkster; Nora Inkster; Dorothy Johnson; Frances Kendrick; Helen Langham; Muriel Lee; Vera Lee; Eva Leslie; Nora Lewis; Helen Malet; Ruth Marks; Dolly Marsden; Beatrice Matthews; Gertrude Matthews; Maud Maxted; Irene Mockett; Annette Moon, Annette Moore; Daphne Morton; Lily Nicholson; Annie Norman; Ethel Owen; Ada Parry-Jones; Mabel Parry-Jones; Beatrice Pascoe; Dilys Pascoe; Kate Patmore, Dorothy Philips; Beatrice Philipps; Grace Peyton; Dorothy Peyton; Lizzie Pollard; Jean Raven; Olive Raven; Muriel Robins; Laura Romer; Nellie Rolfe; Gladys Sargent; Alice Seager; Edith Seaton; Dorothy Shadwell, Dorothy Shew; Mary Snowden, Jessie Stockwell; Mabel Tice; Edith Tomlin, Irene Tuffill; Marian Turnbull, Ethel Vinson; Helen Walker; Kate Wallace; Marion Waller; Ellen Ward; Hilda Warren; Gladys White; Daphne Wickham; Maud Williams

KENT 148, MEREWORTH, WATERINGBURY, AND WEST PECKHAM, was organised in 1913 with the support of Viscountess Falmouth. A hop-picking party, with the Hon. Pamela Boscawen, was conducted for some weeks in September, 1914, to help the cause, and on the outbreak of war the detachment made all arrangements for equipping a Rest Station, if required.

On the opening of Kent 14 Hospital at Hayle Place the detachment received orders to work there, and for some time past have practically taken over the night duty, under a sister. This has only been made possible through the kindness of many friends in lending their motor-cars.

Commandant—Miss E. Moore.
Lady Superintendent—Nurse Keate.
Quartermaster—Miss Swan.

Members.—Ellen Bassett ; Annie Berney ; Elsie Blest ; Rebie Brooks ; Katharine Bunyard ; Lorna Bunyard , Margaret Bunyard ; Cecily Burnaby-Atkins ; Millicent Burnaby-Atkins ; Alexina Chalmers ; Jane Clapson ; Katharine Champion ; Lucy Coe , Alice Goodwin ; Beatrice Goodwin ; Helen Harding ; Rose Harris ; Jane Hooker ; Gwendoline Lemmens ; Dorothea Livett ; Lydia Lockyer ; Dorothea Moore , Katharine Moore ; Mary Ongley ; Nellie Skinner , Daisy Smithers ; Emily Standen , Bertha Stone ; Dorothy Swan , May Swan ; Agnes Wallas ; Ada Warnett ; Ethel Woollett.

KENT 150, WEST MALLING. On the outbreak of war Malling House, West Malling, was kindly offered by Mr. Percy Nevill as a V.A.D. hospital. In November this house, then standing empty, was prepared as a hospital with fifty beds.

Residents in the neighbourhood responded generously with donations, also with loans of equipment. On November 16th the first patients arrived, and since that date the hospital has never been empty. Besides men from the Expeditionary Force and Belgian soldiers, a great number of sick from the local troops have been treated.

Three trained nurses are employed, and the detachment is strongly reinforced by voluntary helpers.

Commandant—MRS. C. WINGFIELD-STRATFORD.
Medical Officer—DR. POPE.
Lady Superintendent—MISS KELLY.
Quartermaster—MISS K. HARDY.

Members.—Edith Adam ; Ethel Adam ; Doris Alston ; Rosalind Blackburne-Mazo ; Violet Cator ; Camillo Doucet ; Cicely Englefield ; Celia Gauntlett ; Norah Hardy ; Ellen Hayton ; Ruth Hayton ; Margaret Lawson ; Florence Pope ; Agnes Roberts ; Madge Roberts ; Isabel Rust ; Isabel Smyth , Margaret Stedman ; Edith Timins ; Ada Viner ; Dorothy Wood ; Elsie Wood ; Marjorie Wood ; Hermione Wingfield-Stratford.

KENT 152, MARGATE. On declaration of war Margate formed two detachments, with Miss M. Mason and Miss Inness as Commandants. Nursing and first aid classes were held. Wanstead Orphan Asylum, Margate branch, was lent by Captain Martin, R.N., as a hospital, with six large wards. A trained nurse is in charge of each ward, with members of the detachments under her. The building was opened on October 14th in conjunction with several private houses, and 110 wounded Belgians were received, and from that time the hospital has been busy, some hundreds of patients having passed through it.

Commandant—Miss M. Inness.

Medical Officers—

Dr. Graham Stewart and Dr. Thomson.

Quartermaster—Miss M. Lloyd.

Members.—Marie Baeten; Ethel Marian Thornton Bobby; Ursula Marian Thornton Bobby; Alice Boldero; Ida Hay Brighurst; Olive Buswell, Mary Callingham; Beatrice Carter; Helen Dorothy Clayton; Edith Cooper; Elwyn Theresa Diehl; Louise Edwards; Hilda Kate Gocher Eveling; Lily Eveling; Mary Finn; Beatrice Mary Giles; Ida May Godfrey; Gertrude Mabel Godwin; Florence Gower; Frances Hadlow; Olga Harrison; Emily Hawkins; Ethel Hews; Phyllis Hill, Eleanor Hobson; Edith Horsley; Annie Keble; Mildred Lamb; Frances Lank; Gwendoline La Trobe; Mary Elizabeth Linnington; Grace Lusby; Edith Mann; Minnie Mandelson; Gertrude Annie McLaughlin; Mary Hilda Mills; Marian Musto; Ada Norton-Smith; Louise Perchard; Frances Mary Pope, Gertrude Pullen; Mabel Gainsborough Ray; Alice Richards; Dorothy Richards; Louise Emma Rogers; Annie Jane Rusholme; Ambrosine Alicia Smithson; Edith Southey; Elsie Spurgwin; Maud Victoria Tappenden; Kate Edith Taylor; Kathleen Taylor; Miss Walker-Smith; Emily Walton; Florence Maud Weir-Rhodes; Ethel Willett.

Kent 154, Tunbridge Wells. Red Cross work originated under the guidance of Miss L. Kemball, with lectures given by Dr. Thurlow, who undertook the training of the members. The detachment was eventually formed at a meeting held at the Grange, when Mrs. Rogers presided as temporary Commandant, Mr. H. Kemball acting as secretary and Mr. S. H. Leeder as treasurer.

N 2

The difficulty of obtaining a house suitable for a hospital was overcome by friends of the cause, who desire to remain anonymous, taking Rust Hall for five years, and giving the detachment use of the same with eventual accommodation for fifty beds. The present Commandant was unanimously elected, Mr. Scott Blair undertook the care of the accounts and Mr. H. M. Caley gave assistance with the care and management of the buildings. Mr. C. Bruce Aitken is honorary solicitor.

Commandant—MISS RACHEL M. ARD.
Medical Officers—
DR. W. C. AYLWARD, DR. B. L. THURLOW.
Lady Superintendent—MISS HODGSON.
Quartermaster—MISS L. KEMBALL.

Members. — Grace Aitken ; Harriet Aitken ; Isabel Barlow ; Alice Mordaunt Barnard ; Mary Bolton ; Kate Bridger ; Alice Bromley ; Annette B. Brooks ; Alice Brown ; Constance Caley ; Marjorie Cass ; Louisa Perceval Clarke ; Isoline Cook ; Beatrice Cook-Hayne ; Mary Coomber ; Ethel Cox ; Caroline Craddock ; Gwendoline Cressey ; Louisa Eliza Crossfield ; Mabel De Mattos ; Rhoda Mary Draper ; Hetty Forbes - Adam ; Lilian M. Foss ; Annie Grier ; Frederica H. Hammond ; Margaret Harding ; Edith Harris ; Mary Hartley ; Daisy Harvey ; Isobel Haynes ; Agnes Hoare ; Mary Hollamby ; Edith Hudson ; Elmira Kemball ; Emma Keys ; Alice Lambart ; Lucy Evelyn Leeder ; Amy Lees ; Eveleen Lees ; Florence Lees ; Ethel Littlewood ; Anna McClean ; Nona McFarlane ; Florence Maunder ; Daisy Mercer ; Florrie Mercer ; Ella Mitchell ; Ella Morgan ; Lilian A. M. Morse ; Elizabeth Nevill ; Violet Overton ; Anne Page ; Mary Panwick ; Maud Pilkington ; Mary C. Pooley ; Florence Maud Poulter ; Evelyn Prescott ; Ellen Price ; Seagram Richardson ; Myddleton Verna Rogers ;

Mabel Sargeaunt; Louisa M. Scattergood; Lydia Ann Shepherd; Catherine Sheppard; Helen Shipton-Green; Alice Smith; Hon. Mary Sommerville; Hon. Florence Starmer; Agnes Stephenson; Margaret Stephenson; Emma Kate Stevens; Myma Symons; Naomi Tabuteau; Ida Taunton; Gertrude Taylor; Ethel Templer; Grace Thompson; Margaret Thorn; Dorothea Tottenham; Jane Turner; Harriett Vaughan; Katherine Waddilove; Elene Waddilove; Marjorie Wade; Una Watson; Margaret Wilde; Rose Withers; Mary Wontner; Doris Wynne.

KENT 156, HAWKHURST, was initiated shortly after the declaration of war, both women's and men's detachments being formed. Lectures and practices were held. On October 14th, 1914, mobilisation took place, and "Lillesden Park," kindly lent by Mr. and Mrs. Loyd, was opened as a hospital with Belgian wounded. The present hospital is "Oakfield."

The equipment was almost entirely supplied by local residents.

During the earlier stages Mrs. Braybrooke and Mrs. Gubbins acted as Commandants, and, with the late Dr. Young, rendered valuable assistance.

Commandant—H. M. BRAYBROOKE.
Medical Officer—DR. STEAD.
Lady Superintendent—SISTER HOLLEY.
Quartermaster—MRS. ROSS-THOMSON.

Members.—Olive Braybrooke; Isabel Butt-Gow; Amy Chatfield; Gladys Cyster; Florence Davis; Hilda Delves; Madge Edwards; Mary Foster; Edith Gormon; Alice Hayward; Violet Heath; Edith Jenner; Lily Kemp; Elsie Mennie, Ellen Morris; Fanny Morris; Kate Pannett; Katharine Percy; Mary Persse; Freda Ross-Thomson;

Mabel Santer ; Cicely Slaughter ; Dorothy Slaughter ; Alice Springett ; Frank Springett ; Helen Springett ; Adelaide Stead ; Selina Ussher ; Evelyn Vaughan-Jenkins ; Frances Williams ; Florence Wilson ; Marjorie Young.

KENT 158, BEXLEY HEATH, was raised in August, 1914. The detachment commenced work in October, when the first convoy of wounded Belgians was received.

The detachment is particularly fortunate in possessing the services of two trained nurses, who give their assistance quite voluntarily : Miss M. Bartlett and Mrs. S. J. Weston, who is Matron of the West Kent Nursing Home, the hospital of the detachment.

Commandant and Medical Officer—
DR. O. SUNDERLAND.
Lady Superintendent—MRS. M. A. COTSELL.
Quartermaster—MISS W. A. R. TYRER.

Members —Ursula Adams ; Florence Berlyn ; Marion Cane ; Alma Chaffey ; Emily Crowe ; Edith Harston ; Ellen Hunnisett ; Alice Jenkins ; Bessie Jenkins ; Edith Jones ; Helen Jones ; Una Lidington ; Hilda Reeves ; Mabel Rix ; Hilda Robinson ; Alix Russell ; Edith Snowden ; Phœbe Windridge.

KENT 160. The Willesborough Women's V.A.D. began its existence in August, 1914 ; the Rev. F. T. Gregg, M.A., Superintendent of the St. John Ambulance Brigade, Willesborough, being the chief mover in its formation.

When the V.A.D. were mobilised it was very soon found that a contingent of Kent 48 could be of great assistance at the Temporary Hospital, Ashford ; and in consequence this detachment acts in that capacity, its services there being greatly appreciated.

Commandant—Miss Fanny M. Pledge.
Lady Superintendent—Mrs. Sims.

Members —Lilian Brake ; Evelyn Devereux-Fleet ; Annie Garner ; Lilian Holdstock ; Edith Holley ; Esther Homewood ; Anna Lilley ; Kathleen Pilcher ; Gertrude Ruck ; Mabel Tomlin ; Alice Wildash ; Mary Wiles.

Recruits —Edith Berry ; Betty Brake ; Milly Elizabeth Brett ; Mabel Buss ; Evelyn Capeling ; Edith Capeling ; May Coleman ; Gladys Chapman , Maggie Crust ; Alice M. Down ; Anah Dines ; Mary Evans ; Rose Harmer ; Minnie Hodges ; Florence Hills ; Elsie Hills ; Louisa Hyland ; Kathleen Merry ; Amy Clara Nicholls ; Alice Elizabeth Noad ; Beatrice Sarkissyan ; Elizabeth Scott ; Jessie Stark ; Lilian Swinerd ; Muriel Thomas ; Muriel Thompson ; Mary White ; Florence Wilde.

Kent 162, Beckenham.

Commandant—Mrs. R. H. Hurlbatt.
Medical Officer—Dr. Curtis.
Quartermaster—Miss Clara Klaber.

Members —Florence Aires ; Breta Bakewell ; Dorothy Bishop ; Marguerite Bluen ; Rita Boot ; Dorothy Buck, Winifred Carey, Adelaide Cleveland, Muriel Coleman ; Clare Curtis, Grace Davis ; Kathleen Dawes ; Maude Derek , Bessie Drughorn ; Nellie Eastwood, Phyllis Fawel, Elsie Firmin ; Gertrude Firmin, Muriel Grose, Elsie Harvey , Margaret Ingram , Evelyn Lemmton , Mary Livingstone ; Amy Marriage , Mary Moreland ; Annie Moser ; Julia Mumford , Lilian Munn ; Rose Neilson, Vera Porter, A. Rogers, Dora Rogers, Leslie Sambrook Freda Smith , Marjorie Soldi ; Winifred Sykes, Johanna Vollers ; Doris Walker Ethel Webb.

HEADQUARTERS

THANKS to the kindness and self-sacrifice of Mrs. Yolland these are still at No. 53 Bromley Common. As stated elsewhere Dr. Cotton acted as County Director most capably until his much-regretted breakdown in health in August. 1914, when Lord Darnley accepted the position of County Director and carried on the duties admirably in close communication with the Chief of Staff. In January, 1915, Lord Darnley was ordered by his physician to take a thorough rest, and Dr. Yolland became Acting County Director until his Lordship's return on May 1st, 1915. The work has progressed continuously and every difficulty has been overcome : all arrangements for future contingencies are complete to the last detail.

Mr. G. Stanley Pond has acted throughout as private secretary to Dr. Yolland, and has helped him in the organisation; Mr. Paul Creswick has been enabled, through the generosity of the Prudential Assurance Co., Ltd., to perform the interesting duties of chief transport officer for the whole county.

The Kent County Committee, to whom so much is due, is constituted as follows :

President :

†THE MARCHIONESS CAMDEN, Bayham Abbey, Lamber-
    hurst, Kent.

Vice-Presidents :

†LADY NORTHCOTE, Eastwell Park, Ashford.
†*LORD HARRIS, Belmont, Faversham.

County Committee :

MRS. WALTER HAY, Manor House, Sevenoaks.
†MRS. A. C. NORMAN, The Rookery, Bromley Common.
†*CHARLES M. HILDER, ESQ., Kirkella, Sevenoaks.
THE HON. MRS. WARD, Squerryes Court, Westerham.
REV. CANON ARNOTT, F.R.C.S., The Rectory, Becken-
    ham.
†LADY BOWER, The Grange, Chislehurst.
THE HON. P. BOWES-LYON, Skeynes Park, Edenbridge.
MRS. PRESTON, Moncks Orchard, West Wickham.
†*ARTHUR N. LUBBOCK, ESQ., The Bassetts, Farn-
    borough.
LOUISA, LADY COHEN, Highfield, Shoreham.
†*J. W. WHEELER-BENNETT, ESQ., Ravensbourne,
    Keston.
†*KENNETH E. CHALMERS, ESQ., Blackbrook, Bickley.
†*R. LEONARD POWELL, ESQ., Heatherbank, Chisle-
    hurst.
†MRS. HOYLE, 24, Park Place, Gravesend.
†SIR GILBERT PARKER, BART., M.P., 20, Carlton House
    Terrace, London, S.W.

THE COUNTESS OF DARNLEY, Cobham Hall, Cobham, Kent.

MRS. E. L. TOMLIN, Angley Park, Cranbrook.

†MRS. CORNWALLIS, Linton Park, Maidstone.

MRS. R. H. STYLE, Boxley House, Maidstone.

†MRS. D'AVIGDOR GOLDSMID, Somerhill, Tonbridge.

VISCOUNTESS HARDINGE, South Park, Penshurst.

MRS. JULIAN, The Old Rectory, Milstead, near Sittingbourne.

THE EARL OF WESTMORLAND, Woodstock Park, Sittingbourne.

MRS. STRANG-STEEL, The Moat, Charing.

MRS. THORNTON DOWN, Spearpoint, Kennington, Ashford.

LORD ROTHERMERE, Hempstead Park, Benenden.

†MRS. BARHAM, Hole Park, Rolvenden.

MAJOR POWELL-COTTON, Quex Park, Birchington.

COLONEL E. T. BUTTANSHAW, Marshview, Hillcrest Road, Hythe.

†LADY DOROTHY RUGGLES BRISE, Hythe.

A. RANDALL-DAVIS, ESQ, M R.C.S., Oaklands, Hythe.

LIEUTENANT-COLONEL S. E. PRATT, I.M.S., Underledge, Hythe.

LADY SEAGER HUNT, 11, Royal Crescent, Ramsgate.

†LADY ROSE WEIGALL, Ramsgate.

MRS. MURRAY SMITH, Westcliff House, Ramsgate.

MRS. PRESCOTT-WESTCAR, Strode Park, Herne.

†LADY GEORGE HAMILTON, Deal Castle, Deal.

LADY PARKER, 20, Carlton House Terrace, London, S.W.

MRS. RANDALL-DAVIDSON, Lambeth Palace, London.

†W. R. FITZHUGH, ESQ., Howitts, Ashford.

†DR. COTTON, Briarfield, Canterbury.

†DR. PRIDEAUX SELBY, Teynham, Kent.

†A. Leon Adutt, Esq., Chelsea Lodge, Margate.

Colonel Sinclair, Barming House, Maidstone.

†*T. Pawley, Esq., 14, Rodway Road, Bromley.

†*Lord Darnley, Cobham Hall, Cobham, Kent.

†*F. Schooling, Esq., Hollydene, Bromley.

Colonel Streatfield, Marlborough House.

D'Avigdor Goldsmid, Esq., Somerhill, Tonbridge.

†The Mayor of Margate (Alderman Booth Reeve), Town Hall, Margate.

†*Geo. Croll, Esq., Millfield, Chislehurst.

†*Geo. Marsham, Esq., Hayle College, Maidstone.

†W. R. Bruce-Culver, Esq , Hope House, Gravesend.

Ex-Officio :

Hon. Secretary and Treasurer : Dr. J. H. Yolland, 53 Bromley Common.

Those whose names are marked † form the Executive Committee under the Chairmanship of Lord Darnley, the County Director

All those marked with a * are Members of the Finance Committee, under the Chairmanship of Mr. J. W. Wheeler-Bennett.

The Assistant County Directors have dealt promptly with all local matters and are allocated thus :

Division I. Dr. Allan, Chislehurst ; Dr. Sterry, Sevenoaks.

II. Dr. Skinner, Strood.

III. Surgeon-Colonel T. Joyce, M.D., Cranbrook; Dr. Travers, Maidstone. Dr. Watson, Tunbridge Wells.

IV. Dr. Prideaux Selby, Sittingbourne.

V. Captain Brandreth Gibbs, Hastings.

VI. Dr. T. Vernon Dodd, Folkestone.

VII. Dr. Frank Brightman, Broadstairs; Surgeon-General F. H. Benson, Walmer.

The County Secretary is Mr. W. R. Bruce-Culver, who, like the Divisional Secretaries, Mr. Alfred Pope, Mrs. Bruce-Culver, Mr. Walter Neve and Dr. J. P. Henderson, have found plenty to do. The county architect and surveyor, Mr. Granville Streatfield, has been of great service. Mr. P. H. Ashton has rendered considerable assistance at headquarters, and, with Messrs. A. Pope, W. W. Gomer, C. D. Quint, Herbert Gurney Smith, Evelyn Gurney Smith, R. Gilliard and other voluntary workers, has made the heavy detail work each day possible of accomplishment. To Dr. E. J. H. Midwinter, Dr. Kirby and Dr. R. A. Shannon sincere acknowledgment is made of much unselfish and valuable help. Mr. T. Pawley, the committee's financial adviser, has had charge of the County Red Cross stores in East Street, Bromley, and has conducted these, in conjunction with Miss Pawley, with success.

Cordial thanks are here expressed to Messrs. Kemp, Sons, Sendell and Co., for acting as Honorary Auditors, and to the Misses Shafto of

Market Square, Bromley, for having undertaken, free of all cost, the whole of the typing for head-quarters.

To all those ladies and gentlemen who have so self-denyingly placed their motor-cars at the disposal of the Chief of Staff his very warm acknowledgments are now made. One and all in Kent, from first to last, have been most generous and public-spirited in assisting the County in its great and successful crusade on behalf of those who have fought so splendidly for all that is best in the British Empire.

PRINTED IN GREAT BRITAIN BY
WM BRENDON AND SON, LTD., PLYMOUTH.

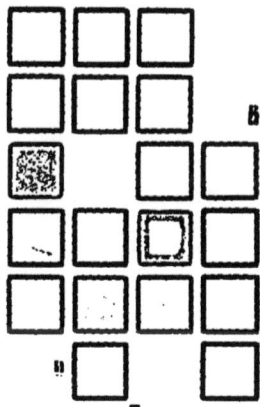

9 781371 863784